CL
ON THE
GRACE OF GOD

KREGEL CLASSIC SERMONS Series

Classic Sermons on the Apostle Paul
Classic Sermons on the Apostle Peter
Classic Sermons on the Attributes of God
Classic Sermons on the Birth of Christ
Classic Sermons on Christian Service
Classic Sermons on the Cross of Christ
Classic Sermons on Faith and Doubt
Classic Sermons on Family and Home
Classic Sermons on the Grace of God
Classic Sermons on Heaven and Hell
Classic Sermons on the Holy Spirit
Classic Sermons on Hope
Classic Sermons on Judas Iscariot
Classic Sermons on the Miracles of Jesus
Classic Sermons on the Names of God
Classic Sermons on Overcoming Fear
Classic Sermons on the Parables of Jesus
Classic Sermons on Praise
Classic Sermons on Prayer
Classic Sermons on the Prodigal Son
Classic Sermons on the Resurrection of Christ
Classic Sermons on Revival and Spiritual Renewal
Classic Sermons on the Second Coming and Other Prophetic Themes
Classic Sermons on the Sovereignty of God
Classic Sermons on Spiritual Warfare
Classic Sermons on Suffering
Classic Sermons on Worship

CLASSIC SERMONS ON THE GRACE OF GOD

Compiled by
Warren W. Wiersbe

Grand Rapids, MI 49501

Classic Sermons on the Grace of God
Compiled by Warren W. Wiersbe

Copyright © 1997 by Kregel Publications. All rights reserved. No part of this book may be reproduced, stored in a retrieval system, or transmitted in any form or by any means—electronic, mechanical, photocopy, recording, or otherwise—without written permission of the publisher, except for brief quotations in printed reviews.

Published by Kregel Publications, a division of Kregel, Inc., P.O. Box 2607, Grand Rapids, MI 49501. Kregel Publications provides trusted, biblical publications for Christian growth and service. Your comments and suggestions are valued.

Cover photo: © 1996, COMSTOCK INC.
Cover and book design: Alan G. Hartman

Library of Congress Cataloging-in-Publication Data

Classic sermons on the grace of God / [compiled by] Warren W. Wiersbe.
      p.   cm.— (Kregel classic sermons series)
  Includes index.
  1. Grace (Theology)—Sermons. 2. Sermons, English.
3. Sermons, American. I. Wiersbe, Warren W. II. Series.
BT761.2.C56   1997   234—dc21   96-45061
                                                                                    CIP

ISBN 0-8254-4077-7

Printed in the United States of America
1 2 3 4 5 / 01 00 99 98 97

CONTENTS

List of Scripture Texts 6
Preface 7
1. The Two Appearings and the
   Discipline of Grace 9
   Charles Haddon Spurgeon
2. The Energy of Grace 29
   John Henry Jowett
3. The Most Magnificent Thing
   in the World 39
   Walter A. Maier
4. The Doctrine of Election 49
   John Calvin
5. Great Guilt No Obstacle to the
   Pardon of the Returning Sinner 63
   Jonathan Edwards
6. The Method of Grace 77
   George Whitefield
7. The Work of Grace 97
   John Daniel Jones
8. The Riches of His Grace 111
   David Martyn Lloyd-Jones
9. The Riches of Grace 127
   Alexander Maclaren
10. How to Be Saved 135
    William E. Sangster
11. Grace Abounding Over Abounding Sin ... 143
    Charles Haddon Spurgeon

LIST OF SCRIPTURE TEXTS

Psalm 25:11, Edwards 63
Jeremiah 6:14, Whitefield 77
Romans 5:20, Spurgeon 143
1 Corinthians 15:10, Jones 97
2 Corinthians 8:9, Maier 39
Ephesians 1:7, Lloyd-Jones 111
Ephesians 1:7–8, Jowett 29
Ephesians 2:7, Maclaren 127
Ephesians 2:8, Sangster 135
2 Timothy 1:9–10, Calvin 49
Titus 2:11–14, Spurgeon 9

PREFACE

THE *KREGEL CLASSIC SERMONS SERIES* is an attempt to assemble and publish meaningful sermons from master preachers about significant themes.

These are *sermons,* not essays or chapters taken from books about themes. Not all of these sermons could be called great, but all of them are *meaningful.* They apply the truths of the Bible to the needs of the human heart, which is something that all effective preaching must do.

While some are better known than others, all of the preachers whose sermons I have selected had important ministries and were highly respected in their day. The fact that a sermon is included in this volume does not mean that either the compiler or the publisher agrees with or endorses everything that the man did, preached, or wrote. The sermon is here because it has a valued contribution to make.

These are sermons about *significant* themes. The pulpit is no place to play with trivia. The preacher has thirty minutes in which to help mend broken hearts, change defeated lives, and save lost souls; he can never accomplish this demanding ministry by distributing homiletical tidbits. In these difficult days we do not need clever pulpiteers who discuss the times; we need dedicated ambassadors who will preach the eternities.

The reading of these sermons can enrich your spiritual life. The studying of them can enrich your skills as an interpreter and expounder of God's truth. However God uses these sermons in your life and ministry, my prayer is that His church around the world will be encouraged and strengthened by them.

WARREN W. WIERSBE

The Two Appearings and the Discipline of Grace

Charles Haddon Spurgeon (1834–1892) is undoubtedly the most famous minister of the nineteenth century. Converted in 1850, he united with the Baptists and soon began to preach in various places. He became pastor of the Baptist church in Waterbeach, England, in 1851, and three years later he was called to the decaying Park Street Church, London. Within a short time the work began to prosper, a new church was built and dedicated in 1861, and Spurgeon became London's most popular preacher. In 1855, he began to publish his sermons weekly; today they make up the fifty-seven volumes of *The Metropolitan Tabernacle Pulpit*. He founded a pastor's college and several orphanages.

This sermon is taken from *The Metropolitan Tabernacle Pulpit*, volume 32. He preached it on Sunday morning, April 4, 1886.

Charles Haddon Spurgeon

1

THE TWO APPEARINGS AND THE DISCIPLINE OF GRACE

> For the grace of God that bringeth salvation hath appeared to all men, teaching us that, denying ungodliness and worldly lusts, we should live soberly, righteously, and godly, in this present world; looking for that blessed hope, and the glorious appearing of the great God and our Saviour Jesus Christ; who gave himself for us, that he might redeem us from all iniquity, and purify unto himself a peculiar people, zealous of good works (Titus 2:11–14).

UPON READING THIS text one sees at a glance that Paul believed in a divine Savior. He did not preach a Savior who was a mere man. He believed the Lord Jesus Christ to be truly man, but he also believed him to be God over all. He therefore uses the striking words: "the glorious appearing of the great God and our Saviour Jesus Christ." There is no appearing of God the Father. There is no such expression in Scripture. The appearing is the appearing of that second person of the blessed Trinity in unity who has already once appeared and who will appear a second time, without a sin offering, to salvation in the latter days. Paul believed in Jesus as "the great God and our Savior." It was his high delight to extol the Lord who once was crucified in weakness. He calls him here, "the great God," thus specially dwelling upon His power, dominion, and glory. This is the more remarkable because he immediately goes on to say, "who gave himself for us, that he might redeem us from all iniquity." He that gave Himself, He that surrendered life itself upon the accursed tree, He that was stripped of all honor and glory and entered into the utmost depths of humiliation was assuredly the great God, notwithstanding all. O friends, if you take away the deity of Christ what in the Gospel is left that is worth the preaching? None but the great God is equal to the work of being our Savior.

We learn also at first sight that Paul believed in a great redemption. "Who gave himself for us, that he might redeem us from all iniquity." That word *redemption* sounds in my ears like a silver bell. We are ransomed, purchased back from slavery, and this at an immeasurable price, not merely by the obedience of Christ nor the suffering of Christ nor even the death of Christ, but by Christ's giving *Himself* for us. All that there is in the great God and Savior was paid down that He might "redeem us from all iniquity." The splendor of the Gospel lies in the redeeming sacrifice of the Son of God, and we shall never fail to put this to the front in our preaching. It is the gem of all the Gospel gems. As the moon is among the stars, so is this great doctrine among all the lesser lights that God has kindled to make glad the night of fallen man. Paul never hesitates. He has a divine Savior and a divine redemption, and he preaches these with unwavering confidence. Oh, that all preachers were like him!

It is also clear that Paul looked upon the appearing of the Savior as a Redeemer from all iniquity as a display of the grace of God. He says, "The grace of God that bringeth salvation hath appeared to all men." In the person of Christ the grace of God is revealed, as when the sun arises and makes glad all land. It is not a private vision of God to a favored prophet on the lone mountain's brow, but it is an open declaration of the grace of God to every creature under heaven—a display of the grace of God to all eyes that are open to behold it. When the Lord Jesus Christ came to Bethlehem and when He closed a perfect life by death upon Calvary, He manifested the grace of God more gloriously than has been done by creation or Providence. This is the clearest revelation of the everlasting mercy of the living God. In the Redeemer we behold the unveiling of the Father's face; what if I say, the laying bare of the divine heart? To repeat the figure of the text, this is the dayspring from on high that has visited us; the Sun that has arisen with healing in His wings. The grace of God has shone forth conspicuously and made itself visible to men of every rank in the person and work of the Lord Jesus. This was not given us because of any deservings on our part; it is a manifestation of free, rich, undeserved grace and of that grace in its fullness. The grace of God has been made manifest to the entire universe in the appearing of Jesus Christ our Lord.

The grand object of the manifestation of divine grace in Christ Jesus is to deliver men from the dominion of evil. The world in Paul's day was sunk in immorality, debauchery, ungodliness, bloodshed, and cruelty of every kind. I do not have time this morning to give you even an outline sketch of the Roman world in which Paul wrote this letter to Titus. We are bad enough now, but the outward manners and customs of that period were simply horrible. The spread of the Gospel has wrought a change for the better. In the apostle's days the favorite spectacles for holiday entertainment were the butcheries of men; such was the general depravity that vices that we hardly dare to mention were defended and gloried in. In the midnight of the world's history our Lord appeared to put away sin. The Lord Jesus Christ, who is the manifestation of the divine grace to men, came into the world to put an end to the unutterable tyranny of evil. His work and teaching are meant to uplift mankind at large and also to redeem His people from all iniquity and to sanctify them to Himself as His peculiar heritage.

Paul looks upon recovery from sin as being a wonderful proof of divine grace. He does not talk about a kind of grace that would leave men in sin and yet save them from its punishment. No, His salvation is *salvation from sin*. He does not talk about a free grace that winks at iniquity and makes nothing of transgression, but of a greater grace by far, which denounces the iniquity and condemns the transgression and then delivers the victim of it from the habit that has brought him into bondage. He declares that the grace of God has shone upon the world in the work of Jesus, in order that the darkness of its sin and ignorance may disappear and the brightness of holiness and righteousness and peace may rule the day. God send us to see these blessed results in every part of the world! God make us to see them in ourselves! May we ourselves feel that the grace of God has appeared to us individually! Our apostle would have Titus know that this grace was intended for all ranks of people, for the Cretians, who were always "liars, evil beasts, slow bellies," and even for the most despised bondslaves, who under the Roman Empire were treated worse than dogs. To each one of us, whether rich or poor, prominent or obscure, the Gospel has come, and its design is that we may be delivered by it from all ungodliness and worldly lusts.

This being the run of the text, I ask you to come closer to it while I try to show how the apostle stimulates us to holiness and urges us to overcome all evil. Firstly, he describes *our position*; secondly, he describes *our instruction*; and, thirdly, he mentions *our encouragements*.

Our Position

The people of God stand between two appearances. In the eleventh verse Paul tells us that "The grace of God that bringeth salvation hath appeared to all men." Then he says, in the thirteenth verse, "Looking for that blessed hope, and the glorious appearing of the great God and our Saviour Jesus Christ." We live in an age that is an interval between two appearings of the Lord from heaven. Believers in Jesus are shut off from the old economy by the first coming of our Lord. The times of man's ignorance God winked at, but now commands all men everywhere to repent. We are divided from the past by a wall of light upon whose forefront we read the words Bethlehem, Gethsemane, Calvary. We date from the birth of the virgin's Son. We begin with *anno Domini*. All the rest of time is before Christ and is marked off from the Christian era. Bethlehem's manger is our beginning. The chief landmark in all time to us is the wondrous life of Him who is the light of the world. We look to the appearing of the grace of God in the form of the lowly one of Nazareth, for our trust is there. We confide in Him who was made flesh and dwelt among us so that men beheld His glory, the glory as of the only begotten of the Father, full of grace and truth. The dense darkness of the heathen ages begins to be broken when we reach the first appearing, and the dawn of a glorious day begins.

Friends, we look forward to a second appearing. Our outlook for the close of this present era is another appearing—an appearing of glory rather than of grace. After our Master rose from the brow of Olivet, His disciples remained for a while in mute astonishment, but soon an angelic messenger reminded them of prophecy and promise by saying, "Ye men of Galilee, why stand ye gazing up into heaven? this same Jesus, which is taken up from you into heaven, shall so come in like manner as ye have seen him go into heaven." We believe that our Lord, in the fullness of time, will descend from heaven with a shout, with the trump of the archangel, and the voice of God.

> The Lord shall come! the earth shall quake;
> The mountains to their centre shake;
> And, withering from the vault of night,
> The stars shall pale their feeble light.

This is the terminus of the present age. We look from *anno Domini*, in which He came the first time, to that greater *anno Domini*, or year of our Lord, in which He shall come a second time in all the splendor of His power to reign in righteousness and break the evil powers as with a rod of iron.

See, then, where we are: we are compassed about, behind and before, with the appearings of our Lord. Behind us is our trust; before us is our hope. Behind us is the Son of God in humiliation; before us is the great God our Savior in His glory. To use an ecclesiastical term, we stand between two epiphanies: the first is the manifestation of the Son of God in human flesh in dishonor and weakness; the second is the manifestation of the same Son of God in all His power and glory. In what a position, then, do the saints stand! They have an era all to themselves that begins and ends with the Lord's appearing.

Our position is further described in the text, if you look at it, as in this present world, or age. We are living in the age that lies between the two blazing beacons of the divine appearings, and we are called to hasten from one to the other. The sacramental host of God's elect is marching on from the one appearing to the other with hasty foot. We have everything to hope for in the last appearing as we have everything to trust to in the first appearing. We have now to wait with patient hope throughout that weary interval which intervenes. Paul calls it "this present world." This marks its fleeting nature. It is present, but it is scarcely future. The Lord may come so soon and thus end it all. It is present now, but it will not be present long. It is but a little time, and He that will come shall come and will not tarry. Now it is this present world; oh, how present it is! How sadly it surrounds us! Yet by faith we count these present things to be unsubstantial as a dream. We look to the things that are not seen and not present as being real and eternal. We pass through this world as people on a pilgrimage. We traverse an enemy's country. Going from one manifestation to another, we are as birds migrating on the wing from one region to another—there is no rest for us by the way. We are to keep ourselves as loose as we can from this country through which we make our pilgrim way, for we are strangers and foreigners, and here we have no continuing city. We hurry through this Vanity Fair; before us lies the Celestial City and the coming of the Lord who is the King thereof. As voyagers cross the Atlantic and so pass from shore to shore, so do we speed over the waves of this ever-changing world to the glory land of the bright appearing of our Lord and Savior Jesus Christ.

Already I have given to you in this description of our position the very best argument for a holy life. If it be so, my friends, you are not of the world even as Jesus is not of the world. If this be so, that before you blazes the supernatural splendor of the Second Advent, and behind you burns the everlasting light of the Redeemer's first appearing, what manner of people ought you to be! If indeed, you be but journeying through this present world, suffer not your hearts to be defiled with its sins; learn not the manner of speech of these aliens through whose country you are passing. Is it not written, "The people shall dwell alone, and shall not be reckoned among the nations"? "Come out from among them, and be ye separate, . . . touch not the unclean thing," for the Lord has said, "I will be a Father unto you, and ye shall be my sons and daughters." They that lived before the coming of Christ had responsibilities upon them, but not such as those that rest upon you who have seen the face of God in Jesus Christ and who expect to see that face again.

You live in light that renders their brightest knowledge a comparative darkness—walk as children of light. You stand between two mornings between which there is no evening. The glory of the Lord has risen upon you once in the incarnation and atonement of your Lord. That light is shining more and more, and soon there will come the perfect day, which shall be ushered in by the Second Advent. The sun shall no more go down, but it shall unveil itself and shed an indescribable splendor upon all hearts that look for it. Put on therefore the "armour of light." What a grand expression! Helmet of light, breastplate of light, shoes of light—everything of light. What a knight must he be who is clad not in steel but in light, light that shall flash confusion on his foes! There ought to be a holy light about you, O believer in Jesus, for there is the appearing of grace behind you and the appearing of glory before you. Two manifestations of God shine upon you. Like a wall of fire the Lord's appearings are around you; there ought to be a special glory of holiness in the midst. "Let your light so shine before men, that they may see your good works, and glorify your Father which is in heaven." That is the position of the righteous, according to my text, and it furnishes a loud call to holiness.

Our Instruction

Our translation runs thus: "The grace of God . . . hath appeared to all men, teaching us that, denying ungodliness and worldly lusts, we should live soberly, righteously, and godly, in this present world." A better translation would be, "the grace of God that bringeth salvation hath appeared to all men, disciplining us in order that we may deny ungodliness and worldly lusts." Those of you who know a little Greek will note that the word that in our version is rendered "teaching" is a scholastic term and has to do with the education of children, not merely the teaching but the training and bringing of them up. The grace of God has come to be a schoolmaster to us, to teach us, to train us, to prepare us for a more developed state. Christ has manifested in His own person that wonderful grace of God which is to deal with us as with sons and daughters and to educate us to holiness and so to the full possession of our heavenly heritage. We are the many sons and daughters who are to be brought to glory by the discipline of grace.

So then, first of all, *grace has a discipline*. We generally think of law when we talk about schoolmasters and discipline, but grace itself has a discipline and a wonderful training power too. The manifestation of grace is preparing us for the manifestation of glory. What the law could not do, grace is doing. The free favor of God instills new principles, suggests new thoughts, and, by inspiring us with gratitude, creates in us love to God and hatred of that which is opposed to God. Happy are they who go to school to the grace of God! This grace of God entering into us shows us what was evil even more clearly than the commandment does. We receive a vital testing principle within, whereby we discern between good and evil. The grace of God provides us with instruction but also with chastisement, as it is written, "As many as I love, I rebuke and chasten." As soon as we come under the conscious enjoyment of the free grace of God, we find it to be a holy rule, a fatherly government, a heavenly training. We find not self-indulgence, much less licentiousness, but on the contrary, the grace of God both restrains and constrains us. It makes us free to holiness and delivers us from the law of sin and death by "the law of the Spirit of life in Christ Jesus."

Grace has its discipline, and *grace has its chosen disciples,* for you cannot help noticing that while the eleventh verse says that, "the grace of God that bringeth salvation hath appeared to all men," yet it is clear that this grace of God has not exercised its holy discipline upon all men, and therefore the text changes its *all men* into *us.* Usually in Scripture when you get a generality you soon find a particularity near it. The text has it, "teaching *us* that, denying ungodliness and worldly lusts, *we* should live soberly, righteously, and godly, in this present world" (italics added). Thus you see that grace has its own disciples. Are you a disciple of the grace of God? Did you ever come and submit yourself to it? Have you learned to spell that word *faith?* Have you childlike trust in Jesus? Have you learned to wash in the laver of atonement? Have you learned those holy exercises that are taught by the grace of God? Can you say that your salvation is of grace? Do you know the meaning of that text, "By grace are ye saved through faith; and that not of yourselves: it is the gift of God"? If so, then you are His disciples, and the grace of God that has appeared so conspicuously has come to discipline you. As the disciples of grace, endeavor to adorn its doctrine. According to the previous verses, even a slave might do this. He might be an ornament to the grace of God. Let grace have such an effect upon your life and character that all may say, "See what grace can do! See how the grace of God produces holiness in believers!" All along I wish to be driving at the point that the apostle is aiming at:

that we are to be holy—holy because grace exercises a purifying discipline and because we are the disciples of that grace.

The discipline of grace, according to the apostle, has three results—denying, living, looking. You see the three words before you.

1. The first is *denying.* When a young man comes to college he usually has much to unlearn. If his education has been neglected, a sort of instinctive ignorance covers his mind with briars and brambles. If he has gone to some faulty school where the teaching is flimsy, his tutor has first of all to fetch out of him what he has been badly taught. The most difficult part of the training of young men is not to put the right thing into them but to get the wrong thing out of them. A man proposes to teach a language in six months, and in the end a great thing is done if one of his pupils is able to forget all his nonsense in six years. When the Holy Spirit comes into the heart, He finds that we know so much already of what it were well to leave unknown. We are self-conceited; we are puffed up. We have learned lessons of worldly wisdom and carnal policy, and these we need to unlearn and deny. The Holy Spirit works this denying in us by the discipline of grace.

What have we to deny? First, we have to deny ungodliness. That is a lesson that many of you have great need to learn. Listen to working people. "Oh," they say, "we have to work hard, we cannot think about God or religion." This is ungodliness! The grace of God teaches us to deny this. We come to loathe such atheism. Others are prospering in the world, and they cry, "If you had as much business to look after as I have, you would have no time to think about your soul or another world. Trying to battle with the competition of the times leaves me no opportunity for prayer or Bible reading. I have enough to do with my daybook and ledger." This also is ungodliness! The grace of God leads us to deny this. We abhor such forgetfulness of God. A great work of the Holy Spirit is to make a man godly, to make him think of God, to make him feel that this present life is not all but that there is a judgment to come wherein he must give an account before God. God cannot be forgotten with impunity. If we treat Him as if He were nothing and leave Him out of our calculations for life, we shall make a fatal mistake. O my hearer, there is a God, and as surely as you live, you are accountable to Him. When the Spirit of God comes with the grace of the Gospel, He removes our inveterate ungodliness and causes us to deny it with joyful earnestness.

We next deny "worldly lusts," that is, the lusts of the present world or age that I described to you just now as coming in between the two appearings. This present age is as full of evil lusts as that in which Paul wrote concerning the Cretians. The lust of the eye, the lust of the flesh, and the pride of life are yet with us. Wherever the grace of God comes effectually, it makes one deny the desires of the flesh; it causes the man who lusted after gold to conquer his greediness; it brings the proud man away from his ambitions; it trails the idler to diligence; it sobers the wanton mind that cared only for the frivolities of life. Not only do we leave these lusts, but we deny them. We have an abhorrence of those things wherein we formerly placed our delight. Our cry is, "What have I to do any more with idols?" To the worldling we say, "These things may belong to you, but as for us, we cannot own them; sin shall no more have dominion over us. We are not of the world, and therefore its ways and fashions are none of ours." The period in which we live shall have no paramount influence over us, for our truest life is with Christ in eternity, our conversation is in heaven. The grace of God has made us deny the prevailing philosophies, glories, maxims, and fashions of this present world. In the best sense we are nonconformists. We desire to be crucified to the world and the world to us. This was a great thing for grace to do among the degraded sensualists of Paul's day, and it is not a less glorious achievement in these times.

2. But then you cannot be complete with a merely negative religion. You must have something positive

and so the next word is *living*—that "we should live soberly, righteously, and godly, in this present world." Observe, friends, that the Holy Spirit expects us to live in this present world, and therefore we are not to exclude ourselves from it. This age is the battlefield in which the soldier of Christ is to fight. Society is the place in which Christianity is to exhibit the graces of Christ. If it were possible for these good sisters to retire into a large house and live secluded from the world, they would be shirking their duty rather than fulfilling it. If all the good men and true were to form a select colony and do nothing else but pray and hear sermons, they would simply be refusing to serve God in His own appointed way. No; you have to live soberly, godly, righteously in this world, such as it is at present. It is of no use for you to scheme to escape from it. You are bound to breast this torrent and buffet all its waves. If the grace of God is in you, that grace is meant to be displayed not in a select and secluded retreat but in this present world. You are to shine in the darkness like a light.

This life is described in a threefold way. You are, first, to live *soberly*—that is, for yourself, "soberly" in all your eating and your drinking and in the indulgence of all bodily appetites—that goes without saying. Drunkards and gluttons, fornicators and adulterers, cannot inherit the kingdom of God. You are to live soberly in all your thinking, all your speaking, all your acting. There is to be sobriety in all your worldly pursuits. You are to have yourself well in hand—you are to be self-restrained. I know some people who are not often sober. I do not accuse them of being drunk with wine, but they are mentally intoxicated. They have no reason, no moderation, no judgment. They are all spur and no rein. Right or wrong, they must have that which they have set their hearts upon. They never look around to take the full bearing of a matter. They never estimate calmly, but with closed eyes they rush on like bulls. Alas for these unsober people! They are not to be depended on, they are everything by turns and nothing long. The one who is disciplined by the grace of God becomes thoughtful, considerate, self-contained; he is no longer tossed about by passion or swayed by prejudice. There is only one insobriety into which I pray we may fall, and truth to say, that is the truest sobriety. Of this the Scripture says, "Be not drunk with wine, wherein is excess; but be filled with the Spirit." When the Spirit of God takes full possession of us, then we are borne along by His sacred energy and are filled with a divine enthusiasm that needs no restraint. Under all other influences, we must guard ourselves against yielding too completely, that thus we may live "soberly."

As to one's business associates the believer lives *righteously*. I cannot understand that Christian who can do a dirty thing in business. Craft, cunning, overreaching, misrepresentation, and deceit are no instruments for the hands of godly people. I am told that my principles are too angelic for business life—that a person cannot be a match for one's business associates in trade if he is too Puritanic. Others are up to tricks, and he will be ruined if he cannot trick them in return. O my dear hearers, do not talk in this way. If you mean to go the way of the Devil, say so, and take the consequences; but if you profess to be servants of God, deny all partnership with unrighteousness. Dishonesty and falsehood are the opposites of godliness. A Christian person may be poor, but he must live righteously. He may lack sharpness, but he must not lack integrity. A Christian profession without uprightness is a lie. Grace must discipline us to righteous living.

Toward God we are told in the text that we are to be *godly*. Everyone who has the grace of God in him indeed and of a truth will think much of God and will seek first the kingdom of God and His righteousness. God will enter into all his calculations, God's presence will be his joy, God's strength will be his confidence, God's providence will be his inheritance, God's glory will be the chief end of his being, God's law the guide of his conversation. Now, if the grace of God, which has appeared so plainly to all has really come with its sacred discipline upon us, it is teaching us to live in this threefold manner.

3. Once more, there is *looking*, as well as living. One work of the grace of God is to cause us to be "looking for that blessed hope, and the glorious appearing of the great God and our Saviour Jesus Christ." What is that "blessed hope"? Why, first, that when He comes we shall rise from the dead, if we have fallen asleep, and that, if we are alive and remain, we shall be changed at His appearing. Our hope is that we shall be approved of Him and shall hear Him say, "Well done, good and faithful servant." This hope is not of debt but of grace. Though our Lord will give us a reward, it will not be according to the law of works. We expect to be like Jesus when we shall see Him as He is. When Jesus shines forth as the sun, "then shall the righteous shine forth as the sun in the kingdom of their Father." Our gain by godliness cannot be counted down into the palm of the hand. It lies in the glorious future, and yet to faith it is so near that at this moment I almost hear the chariot of the Coming One. The Lord comes, and in the coming of the Lord lies the great hope of the believer, his great stimulus to overcome evil, his main incentive to perfect holiness in the fear of the Lord. Oh, to be found blameless in the day of the manifestation of our Lord! God grant us this! Do you not see how the discipline of the doctrine of grace runs toward the separating of us from sin and the making us to live to God?

Our Encouragements

In this great battle for right and truth and holiness, what could we do, my brethren and my sisters, if we were left alone? But *our first encouragement is that grace has come to our rescue,* for in the day when the Lord Jesus Christ appeared among men, He brought for us the grace of God to help us to overcome all iniquity. He that struggles now against inbred sin has the Holy Spirit within him to help him. He that goes forth to fight against evil in others by preaching the Gospel has that same Holy Spirit going with the truth to make it like a fire and like a hammer. I would ground my weapons and retreat from a fight so hopeless were it not that the Lord of Hosts is with us—the God of Jacob is our refuge. The grace of God that brings salvation from sin has flashed forth conspicuously like the lightning that is seen from one part of the heaven to the other, and our victory over darkness is insured. However hard the conflict with evil, it is not desperate. We may hope on and hope ever. A certain warrior was found in prayer, and when his king sneezed, he answered that he was pleading with his majesty's august ally. I question whether God is the ally of anybody when he goes forth with gun and sword. But in using those weapons that are "not carnal, but mighty through God to the pulling down of strong holds," we may truly reckon upon our august ally. Speak the truth, man, for God speaks with you! Work for God, woman, for God works in you to will and to do of His own good pleasure. The appearance of the grace of God in the person of Christ is encouragement enough to those who are under the most difficult circumstances and have to contend for righteousness against the deadliest odds. Grace has appeared, wherefore let us be of good courage!

A second encouragement is that another appearing is coming. He who bowed His head in weakness and died in the moment of victory is coming in all the glory of His endless life. Do not question it, the world is not going to darken into an eternal night. The morning comes as well as the night, and though sin and corruption abound, and the love of many grows cold, these are but the tokens of His near advent who said that it would be so before His appearing. The right with the might and the might with the right shall be—as surely as God lives, it shall be so. We are not fighting a losing battle. The Lord must triumph. Oh, if His suffering life and cruel death had been the only appearing, we might have feared—but it is not. It is but the first and the prefatory part of His manifestation. He comes! He comes! None can hinder His coming! Every moment brings Him nearer; nothing can delay His glory. When the hour shall strike He shall appear in the majesty of God to put an end to the dominion of sin and bring in endless peace. Satan shall be bruised under our feet shortly; wherefore comfort one another with these words, and then prepare for further battle. Grind your swords, and be ready for close fighting! Trust in God and keep your powder dry. Ever this our war cry, "He must reign." We are looking for the appearing of the great God and Savior Jesus Christ.

Another encouragement is that we are serving a glorious Master. The Christ whom we follow is not a dead prophet like Muhammad. Truly we preach Christ crucified, but we also believe in Christ risen from the dead, in Christ gone up on high, in Christ soon to come a second time. He lives, and He lives as the great God and our Savior. If indeed you are soldiers of such a Captain, throw fear to the winds. Can you be cowards when the Lord of Hosts leads you? Dare you tremble when at your head is the Wonderful, the Counselor, the Mighty God, the Everlasting Father, the Prince of Peace? The trumpet is already at the lips of the archangel; who will not play the man? The great drum that makes the universe to throb summons you to action.

> Stand up, stand up for Jesus,
> Ye soldiers of the cross;
> Lift high his royal banner,
> It must not suffer loss.

His cross is the old cross still and none can overthrow it. Hallelujah, hallelujah to the name of Jesus!

Then come the tender thoughts with which I finish, the memories of what the Lord has done for us to make us holy: "Who gave himself for us." Special redemption, redemption with a wondrous price—"who gave himself for us." Put away that trumpet and that drum, take down the harp and gently touch its sweetest strings. Tell how the Lord Jesus loved us and gave

Himself for us. O sirs, if nothing else can touch our hearts this must: "Ye are not your own. . . . ye are bought with a price."

And He gave Himself for us with these two objects: first, redemption, that He might redeem us from all iniquity, that He might break the bonds of sin asunder and cast the cords of depravity far from us. He died—forget not that—died that your sins might die, died that every lust might be dragged into captivity at His chariot wheels. He gave Himself for you that you might give yourselves for Him.

Again, He died that He might purify us—purify us to Himself. How clean we must be if we are to be clean to Him! The holy Jesus will only commune with that which He has purified after the manner of His own nature—purified to Himself. He has purified us to be wholly His. No human hand may use the golden cup, no human incense may burn in the consecrated censer. We are purified to Him, as the Hebrew would put it, to be His *segullah,* His peculiar possession. The translation *peculiar people* is unfortunate, because *peculiar* has come to mean odd, strange, singular. The passage really means that believers are Christ's own people, His choice and select portion. Saints are Christ's crown jewels, His box of diamonds, His very, very, very own. He carries His people as lambs in His bosom. He engraves their names on His heart. They are the inheritance to which He is the heir, and He values them more than all the universe beside. He would lose everything else sooner than lose one of them. He desires that you who are being disciplined by His grace should know that you are altogether His. You are Christ's men and women. You are each one to feel, "I do not belong to the world. I do not belong to myself. I belong only to Christ. I am set aside by Him for Himself only, and His I will be." The silver and the gold are His, and the cattle upon a thousand hills are His, but He makes small account of them, "the Lord's portion is his people."

The apostle finishes up by saying that we are to be a people "zealous of good works." Would to God that all

Christian men and women were disciplined by divine grace until they became zealous for good works! In holiness, zeal is sobriety. We are not only to approve of good works and speak for good works, but we are to be red-hot for them. We are to be on fire for everything that is right and true. We may not be content to be quiet and inoffensive, but we are to be zealous of good works. Oh, that my Lord's grace would set us on fire in this way! There is plenty of fuel in the church; what is wanted is fire. A great many very respectable people are, in their sleepy way, doing as little as they can for any good cause. This will never do. We must wake up. Oh, the quantity of ambulance work that Christ's soldiers have to do! One half of Christ's army has to carry the other half. Oh, that our brethren could get off the sick list! Oh, that all of us were ardent, fervent, vigorous, zealous! Come, Holy Spirit, and quicken us! We may not go about to get this by our own efforts and energies, but God will work it by His grace. Grace given us in Christ is the fountainhead of all holy impulse. O heavenly grace, come like a flood at this time and bear us right away!

Oh, that those of you who have never felt the grace of God may be enabled to believe in the Lord Jesus Christ as to His first appearing! Then, trusting in His death upon the cross, you will learn to look for His second coming upon the throne, and you will rejoice therein. To His great name be glory forever and ever! Amen.

NOTES

The Energy of Grace

John Henry Jowett (1864–1923) was known as "the greatest preacher in the English-speaking world." He was born in Yorkshire, England. He was ordained into the Congregational ministry, and his second pastorate was at the famous Carr's Lane Church, Birmingham, where he followed the eminent Dr. Robert W. Dale. From 1911 to 1918, he pastored the Fifth Avenue Presbyterian Church, New York City; from 1918 to 1923, he ministered at Westminster Chapel, London, succeeding G. Campbell Morgan. He wrote many books of devotional messages and sermons.

This message is taken from *Apostolic Optimism,* published in 1930 by Richard R. Smith, Inc., New York.

John Henry Jowett

2

THE ENERGY OF GRACE

In whom we have redemption through his blood, the forgiveness of sins, according to the riches of his grace; wherein he hath abounded toward us in all wisdom and prudence (Ephesians 1:7–8).

"ACCORDING TO THE riches of his grace; wherein he hath abounded toward us." I recently pronounced the words aloud as I walked alone in a beautiful twilight by the fringe of the incoming sea. The truth in nature seemed to recognize the truth in revelation. They appeared to grasp hands. Deep called to deep, and they offered each other the help of a mutual interpretation. It is wonderful how frequently an old and unsuggestive word will glow with vivid significance when proclaimed in new surroundings! "Let your speech be always with grace, seasoned with salt." I read these words when standing upon a bold headland on a day of warm and genial light with a little breeze playing through it, which was burdened with the essence of the brine. As the one offered itself as commentary upon the other, I knew the meaning of sanctified conversation, intercourse that is warm and genial and cheering and yet bracing and invigorating by reason of the truth-laden spirit which blows from the infinite.

"Always with grace, yet seasoned with salt." "Renewed by his spirit in the inner man." The word repeated itself to me with acquired emphasis as I emerged from a sultry glebe where the atmosphere had been close and stagnant and oppressive, and I stood in the pure, cool, moving air of the heights. "Refreshed by his spirit in the inner man." And once again I read the words of my text to the accompaniment of the jubilant roar and the majestic advance of the incoming tide.

"According to the riches of his grace; wherein he hath abounded toward us"! The onrush of the ocean seemed to get into the words. I could feel a magnificent tidal flow in the great evangel. The infinite was moving in determined fullness. The grace of the Eternal was rolling toward the race in a wealthy and glorious flood. "According to the riches of His grace; wherein He hath abounded toward us."

I am grateful for this comment of the ocean tide. I am grateful for its suggestion of unspeakable energy in the ministry of grace. Grace is too commonly regarded as a pleasing sentiment, a sofa disposition, a welcome feeling of cozy favor entertained toward us by our God. The interpretation is ineffective and inevitably cripples the life in which it prevails. Grace is more than a smile of good nature. It is not the shimmering face of an illumined lake; it is the sunlit majesty of an advancing sea. It is a transcendent and ineffable force, the outgoing energies of the redeeming personality of God washing against the polluted shores of human need.

How inclined we are to think meanly and narrowly of spiritual ministries. How we belittle and impoverish their dominion! We think more largely concerning the palpable ministries of the material world. How spaciously we think of the empire of electrical force, the subtle fluid that annihilates space. But when we turn to finer subtleties still, our thinking is inclined to move more timidly and with a severely circumscribed range. Turn the mind upon itself. Here is a spiritual entity. What is *thought?* Is it only a faint effluence of the mind that remains locked up within the limits of one's own personality? Is thought only a perfume—or a stench—that dies away within the confines in which it is born? Or is thought an energy, more potent and pervasive than the electrical fluid, disregarding the limits of personality and moving irresistibly and inevitably from life to life? What if we cannot dam it up? What if thought will be out and, whether we will or not, becomes an operative factor in the common life? That is the larger and sounder way of regarding spiritual essences. Thought is energy. Purpose is energy. Goodwill is energy. And even though we withhold from them the vehicles of speech and act, they will nevertheless express themselves, by the very reason of their being, as influential ministers in human life.

Now lift up the argument to a still higher plane. I gaze into the wealthy content of this spacious word *grace*. Whatever else it may mean or does not mean, it includes thought and purpose and goodwill and love. We do it wrong, and therefore maim ourselves, if we esteem it only as a perfumed sentiment, a favorable inclination, and not as a glorious energy moving toward the race with the fullness and majesty of the ocean tide. Wherever I turn in the Sacred Book I find the mystic energy at work. It operates in a hundred diverse ways, but in every instance it works and energizes as an unspeakable force.

Let me cull a little handful of examples from the old Book. "Let each man do according as he hath purposed in his heart. . . . And God is able to make all grace abound unto you" (RV). Do you catch the swift and vital connection? Let each man *do*, and God will make grace abound. Grace is the dynamic of endeavor! We have "good hope through grace." We have good hope! The lamp is kept burning. The cheery light does not die out in the life. All the rooms are lit up. Our confidence fails not. We have good hope through grace. Grace is the nourisher of optimism. "Singing with grace in your hearts." How beautiful the relation and succession—grace in the heart—a song in the mouth! Grace is the spring of a grateful contentment. "It is a good thing that the heart be established with grace." There we are, away in the basement among the foundations of the life, establishing the heart with grace. Grace is the secret energy of a fortified will. And so in countless other places I find the grace of God working away in human life as an energy whose operations are as manifold as the ministries of the light.

And now the apostle tells me that this redeeming, energizing effluence flows toward the race in all the spacious plenitude of a flood. Grace does not flow from a half-reluctant and partially reconciled God, like the scanty and uncertain movements of a brook in time of drought. It comes in oceanic fullness. It comes in riches of mercy; "riches of his goodness and forbearance and long suffering"; "riches of glory." "According to the riches of his grace; wherein he hath abounded toward us." "O the depth of the riches both of the wisdom and knowledge of God!"

> Thy goodness and Thy truth to me,
>   To every soul abound,
> A vast unfathomable sea,
>   Where all our thoughts are drowned,
> Its streams the whole creation reach,
>   So plenteous in the store:
> Enough for all, enough for each,
>   Enough for evermore.

Now in my text the energies of grace are more particularly discovered in their relationship to sin. "Forgiveness of sins, according to the riches of His grace." The word *grace* is not a prevalent word in modern speech, and its rare occurrence may be explained by the partial disappearance of the word *sin* from our vocabulary. If we exile the one we shall not long retain the other. Grace haunts the place where pangs are endured and tears are shed because of the sense of indwelling sin. "Where sin abounded, grace did much more abound." But you may ransack the books of the passing day, and though the life depicted moves among many crookednesses and perversities and uncleannesses, there is little or no suggestion of the sense of sin. I do not say it is not there, but men are unfavorably disposed toward the word and are inclined to banish it from their vocabulary.

Sin is a word whose familiar significances are like sharp fangs, and they bite deep into the life. Men are now very busy attempting to draw the teeth of the old rodent and to leave him with a pair of harmless gums. We are busy creating easier and less distressing phrases, phrases without teeth, that we can apply to our perversities and deformities without occasioning us any pain. The prevalent philosophy is a little favorable to our much-sought-for deliverance. You know the welcome opiates it offers to our uneasy consciousness. It declares that what is called sin is only the result of imperfect knowledge. But the philosophy does not build itself upon the facts of common experience. Where ignorance reigns, the sense of sin does not prevail. Where there is a sense of sin a man is conscious that he had the requisite knowledge. Where a man can say, "I did it ignorantly," his inner life may be distressed but not with the consciousness of guilt. For him, in this relationship, sin does not exist.

"Sin is inevitable," says another prevalent philosophy, "so long as we are bound to a sensuous body. Our union with the flesh is the necessary occasion of all our sin." But all sin is not the necessary accompaniment of sense. If men were to be stripped of their bodies today, the realm of sin would still remain, envy would remain, and malice and wrath, and so would thought and desire and will. No, these philosophic extenuations do not root themselves in the well-recognized facts of the individual life and so will not bring any permanent peace to men. What philosophy and personal inclination are disposed to extenuate, the Christian religion seeks to deepen and revive. Its purpose and endeavor is not to abate the uneasy sense of sin but to drive the teeth into still more sensitive parts. There is no mincing, apologizing delicacy in the way in which it describes the natural conditions of my life. It makes no attempt at discovering more favorable considerations that will set me more at ease. Its revealing sentences are clear and uncompromising. "Sin . . . dwelleth in me." I have opened the door of my life and have invited sin to be my guest and accept my hospitality. Sin reigns in me. The guest has become the master and determines the arrangements of the house. I am the bondslave of sin. Sin is not merely my guest, not only my master, he is my tyrant, with his heavy hand upon the neck, holding me down, thrusting me along his own determined way. I am dead in sin; I am become a mere chattel, my tyrant's dead implement used in the evil ministry of the Devil. I am dead in sin, not a finely rigged and self-determining boat with power to encounter adverse winds and to ride upon the storm, but a piece of dead driftwood, a poor hull, with its power of self-initiative and self-direction gone, the pitiless prey of the hostile wind and the engulfing waves. "Dead in trespasses and sins." That is the scriptural indictment of the sin-possessed man.

Indictment, do I say? I recall the word; it is the scriptural portrait of the sin-ridden life. I say that the common heart of man acknowledges the accuracy of it and brushes all attempted extenuations on one side as being beside the mark and having no relevancy and pertinacity to man's appalling need. "Cleanse me from its *guilt* and *power*." Guilt and power! Those are the two deadly facts of sin, and they are witnessed to in the common life. I look around and within me, and the evidence abounds. If I interpret my own heart aright, the sense of guilt is signified in more ways than by audible confession and sighs. The sense of guilt has a very varied wardrobe. It is not always found in sackcloth and ashes, lowly kneeling, or smiting the breast. I have seen it dressed as flippancy; I have known it to put on the guise of jaunty carelessness; I have known it issued as forced laughter; I have seen it evidenced in a passionate recoil against religion.

John Wesley tells us in his incomparable journal that when he was about twenty-two, before he had felt the tidal powers of redeeming grace, he took up and read Kempis's *The Christian's Pattern*. He began to "see that true religion was seated in the heart, and that God's law extended to all our thoughts as well as words and actions. I was, however, very angry with Kempis for being too strict." Is that a surprising consequence? I thought that this enlarged vision of the searching demands of God's law would have drawn him to his knees in humble and contrite confession of sin!

"I was, however, very angry with Kempis for being too strict." The consciousness of guilt emerged in the guise of anger in a heated recoil from the man who had searched him in the inward parts.

I do not look merely for kneeling and tearful worshipers when I want evidence of the consciousness of sin. I can see it in loud living, in violent and sensational pleasures, in proudly assured indifference, in the anger aroused by august ideals, in passionate aversions to the teachings of evangelical religion. To rummage among the secrets of the heart and to survey the symptoms of the external life is to find abounding witness that man is held in dark and cruel servitude by the guilt and power of sin.

And now to this sin-burdened and sin-poisoned race there flows, in infinite plenitude, the riches of His grace. What is the ministry of the heavenly energy? What are the contents of the gracious flood? The inspiring evangel of the text gathers itself around three emphases. I am told that when grace possesses the life, it brings in its resources a threefold power. It brings "redemption," the powers of liberation; it brings "wisdom," the power of illumination; it brings "prudence," the power of practically applying the illumination to the manifold exigencies of the common life.

Let us feast our eyes on the wealthy program. Grace flows around the life in powers of liberation. It sets itself to deal both with the guilt and the power of sin, and it removes the one and subdues the other. The Bible seems to exhaust all available figures in seeking to make it clear to men how effective and absolute is the liberation accomplished by grace.

Here is a little handful gathered in a field in which they abound. "Your sins may be blotted out!" Blotted out! It is the same word that is used in another beautiful promise: "God shall wipe away all tears." Your sins shall be wiped away! Just as you may wipe a tear away from the eye of a child and its place is taken by sunny light and no print remains of the grievous presence, so our Father will wipe away our sins by the energies of His grace. "The Lamb of God, which taketh away the sin of the world." Taketh away! It is the word which is used in another familiar phrase: they found the stone "taken away." He takes away the sin of the world—the huge, unliftable stone, before which we stood in paralyzing despair—He takes it away. "He shall wash away your sin. The ministry of soft and genial water! When a little child with slightly afflicted eyes awakens in the morning and finds that her eyes are fastened by the clog that has accumulated through the night, the mother takes some balmy water and gently washes away the ill cement, and the little one opens her eyes upon the morning light. And when the glue of guilt has gathered about the powers of my life, and holds their activities in depressing and fearful servitude, the stringent, healing energy of grace washes away the encumbrance, and the powers of the soul exult in newly discovered liberty and light. He shall wash away your sin.

And so I might proceed with the wealthy array of Scriptural figures. Our sins are to be blotted out; they are to be taken away; they are to be washed away; they are to be covered; they are to be purged. All this wealth of metaphor is intended to proclaim the completeness of the emancipation accomplished by these marvelous energies of grace. We have redemption, even the forgiveness of sin, "according to the riches of His grace; wherein he hath abounded toward us."

But this by no means exhausts the contents of the ministry of grace. The grace that liberates also illuminates. The grace that brings redemption also confers wisdom. Our opened eyes are to be fed and feasted with ever more glorious unveilings of the Eternal. We are to obtain more and more spacious conceptions of truth, richer and profounder knowledge of God. Oh, what vistas of knowledge are promised to the grace-filled life! "That ye may know what is the hope of his calling, and what the riches of the glory of his inheritance in the saints." "To know the love of Christ which passeth knowledge." "That ye may know!" That ye may *know!* That is the reiterated emphasis of the word of promise. The grace that lifts up also lights up. The new birth is succeeded by new visions, and the new visions refine and beautify the life. That is the ministry of all vision. The vision soaks into the life and colors it with its own hue. "We all, with open face *beholding* . . . the glory of the Lord, are *transformed* [RV] *into* the same image" (italics added). The nature of our contemplation determines the quality and color of our lives.

Redemption, power of liberation! Wisdom, power of illumination! And prudence, power of fruitful application, power to apply the eternal to the transient, power to bring the vision to the task, the revelation to the duty, the truth to the trifle. Grace will not confine its operations to the clouds. It will flow up into the practicalities and prudences of common daily life. It will prove itself the dynamic of the ordinary day. There is many a man possessed of knowledge who does not know how to apply it. But grace does not leave a man in the vacuity and impotence of mere theory. The gift of grace is not only the gift of vision, but the gift of power to realize the vision in the humdrum concerns of the unattractive life.

Now how do we come into the sweep of the marvelous effluence of the grace of God? "In whom we have." That is the standing ground. I know no other. To be in Him, in the Christ, is to be in the abiding place of this superlative energy. To be associated with the Savior, by faith, in the fellowship of spiritual communion, is to dwell at the springs of eternal life.

> Jesus sought me when a stranger,
>   Wandering from the fold of God;
> He, to rescue me from danger,
>   Interposed His precious blood.
>
> Oh, to grace how great a debtor
>   Daily I'm constrained to be!
> Let thy grace, Lord, like a fetter,
>   Bind my wandering heart to Thee.

The Most Magnificent Thing in the World

Walter A. Maier (1893–1950) was known around the world as the speaker on *The Lutheran Hour,* heard over more than a thousand radio stations. Many of his faithful listeners did not realize that this effective communicator was also professor of Old Testament and Semitic Languages at Concordia Seminary in St. Louis. It was said the Maier spent one hour in preparation for each minute that he spoke on the radio. Many of his radio sermons were published in volumes still treasured by those who appreciate good preaching.

This sermon is found in *The Lutheran Hour,* published by Concordia Publishing House, St. Louis, in 1931.

Walter A. Maier

3
THE MOST MAGNIFICENT THING IN THE WORLD

> Ye know the grace of our Lord Jesus Christ, that, though he was rich, yet for your sakes he became poor, that ye through his poverty might be rich (2 Corinthians 8:9).

WHAT IS THE most beautiful, the most wonderful, the most magnificent thing in this world? Can it be sought and found in the entrancing splendor of nature, in the rugged grandeur of rock-bound, snowcapped mountains that etch their majestic peaks against the evening background of the flaming skies, or in the sylvan silence of cathedral-like forests where stately sentinels of leafy green lift men's gaze from earth to heaven? No; there is something infinitely more beautiful, more wonderful, more magnificent than all this; for the earth and all that is in it is but the footstool of One whose divine power has given us a far nobler and more exalted height of wondrous beauty and magnificence.

We ask again, then: Is this to be sought and found among men in the exquisite forms of physical beauty or in the deeper treasures of the inner life? Many there are who would answer, "Yes," and point us to the charm of blemishless beauty or to the deep and powerful emotion of love—the love of husband and wife, the love of parents and children, the love of friendship, the love of patriotism, love in its purest and noblest human forms. But again comes the echo: There is something more beautiful, far more wonderful, inexpressibly more magnificent than all this. We read in the Record of Truth of One who is "fairer than the children of men." We hear of a greater love—that of laying down one's life for one's friends. And He who told us of this love Himself laid down His life not only for His friends, but for

His enemies, to reveal to us by that very self-sacrifice the unparalleled height of immeasurable magnificence, the grace of God in Jesus Christ.

Unparalleled and immeasurable, I say, because the human intellect, even with its most advanced achievements, lacks every capacity to understand adequately the depth and the meaning of that love which the great apostle describes when he tells us: "Ye know the grace of our Lord Jesus Christ, that, though he was rich, yet for your sakes he became poor, that ye through his poverty might be rich."

The Magnificent Riches of Christ

Note how clearly these words point to the magnificent riches of Jesus Christ in these opening words, "though he was rich." And oh, that it were possible to picture to you the limitless munificence of your Savior! The national wealth of these United States is estimated at about four hundred billion dollars. The wealth of all the nations of the whole earth and of all ages would aggregate staggering totals of inconceivable billions. But if we could take the sum total of all the wealth of which men have ever known and multiply it a thousandfold, all this would be a mere bagatelle compared with the depth of the riches over which our Lord, as the eternal God, held undisputed sway. He was rich, rich in the resources and wealth of the entire universe that is His; rich in the exercise of all power in heaven and in earth, in the control of the myriads of constellations beyond the searching gaze of the most penetrating telescope; rich in the direction of the shifting tides of the oceans, in the shaping of human affairs as they are molded into history. He was rich in the majestic adoration of the heavenly legions that encircle the throne of His divinity; rich in the glory and purity of His divine sinlessness; rich in truth, in wisdom, and in justice. But—endless praise to His holy name!—He was rich in love, in mercy, in grace, toward a corroding and decaying world that had spurned the guidance of God—so rich that, as unfathomable as it may be to our human reason, He showed the depth of His divine compassion for human souls by the magnificence of that tremendous sacrifice of which our text continues to speak when it adds, "yet for your sakes He became poor."

The Magnificent Sacrifice of Christ

I sometimes wonder how many there are who can adequately measure the abject poverty of our Lord in the depths of His humiliation when He humbled Himself to death, even the death of the cross. It is true, we speak of His holy cross with reverence and love. We mold it into symbols of gold and precious metals; we place it high upon the spires of our churches, above all the noise and grime of our earthbound, daily existence; we have made the cross the greatest of all human symbols. Yet how little we sometimes comprehend the love of Him who so inexpressibly impoverished Himself and finally died upon the accursed tree!

And what a death it was! No matter under what circumstances the Grim Reaper may come, there is always a crushing pain and the sorrow of anguish that arises from grief-torn hearts when our loved ones are called home by God. Even if we surround them with all the comforts that money and medical science can offer, even if we give them every possible attention, sit by their deathbeds to wipe the fevered brow and pray with all the fervor of which the human heart is capable, even then there is that numb pain, that depressing sorrow, that indescribable grief which always comes with death.

But how immeasurably more intense was our Savior's crucifixion! a mode of capital punishment so horrible that it was not recognized by the church of the Old Testament; so degrading that, as a Latin author tells us, it was a punishment inflicted upon slaves; so painful that it has universally been considered one of the most excruciating modes of torture ever known.

But this does not explain even partially the fullness of the infinite grace of Christ and the appalling depths of His self-assumed poverty. There have been men who have suffered long and intensely and who have died for others, noble and heroic martyrs to the cause of their country. We think, for example, of Arnold von Winkelried who gathered the long spears of the Austrian phalanx and plunged them into the warm lifeblood of his heart to make way for his Tyrolian fatherland. With the message of Armistice Day still lingering with us, we think of unnamed and unknown heroes who have suffered and bled and died in order to insure religious and political freedom to us and to our posterity. We think of the noblest examples of such heroic sacrifice, but when we compare all this with the self-sacrifice of the Lord Jesus, it dwindles into less than obscurity. For on the cross, deserted by God and by men, is One who in His marred and tortured body bears the crushing weight of all the sins that have ever been committed throughout the long annals of history. Here, in the poverty of Christ, is the greatest spectacle of love that men have ever beheld or ever will behold—"not that we loved God, but that he loved us, and sent his Son to be the propitiation for our sins." Here, with His divine arms outstretched as though He would embrace sinful humanity in its overwhelming totality, is God's answer to the plea of mankind for the forgiveness of sins, for the power to counteract evil, for the ability to rise up over the enshrouding gloom of death. Here, in the abysmal poverty of Christ, is the magnificence of grace—pure, saving, sanctifying grace.

The Magnificent Blessing of Christ

Then think of the universality of grace that is embraced in these three words, "for your sakes." We have become more internationally minded than any previous generation. Yet in spite of all the activities of our various world congresses and leagues, no human plan or arrangement has ever begun to make the approach to that universal appeal that comes with the Gospel message of grace. We know that President Chiang Kai-shek recently followed the example of three million Chinese by embracing Christianity; can you conceive of a president of the United States accepting Confucianism? We know that four million of Mother India's children have accepted the Christ as their Savior, but the isolated Westerners who have adopted Buddhism or Brahmanism are only the abnormal exceptions. Is there anyone in my audience from coast to coast tonight who can name a half dozen normal, healthy-minded Americans who believe in Muhammad's Koran, with its background of Oriental passion and voluptuousness and its heaven of sensual attractions? But hundreds of thousands of Muhammadans have been brought to Christ. Why all this? Is it not because the message of the great humiliation of Christ *for your sakes* is the promise that holds out hope to every child of the human race regardless of racial, national, or geographical distinctions?

The magnificence of the grace of Christ is seen just in this, that, whenever a man looks up to that cross and beholds those arms outstretched to receive him, it does not matter where that man comes from or what his education is, whether he is an illiterate or an intellectual leader. It does not matter what his social standing is, be it that of a criminal behind penitentiary bars or that of one who has ascended to the pinnacle of preeminence in the affairs of the world. It does not matter what his financial status is, whether he be one of the large army of the unemployed who live on from day to day in dread anticipation of the rigors of the coming winter or whether he be one whose Midas touch has heaped up a fabulous reserve of golden treasures. It does not matter what a man's color or his culture or his reputation or his age or his influence may be, when he comes to that cross and acknowledges that Christ as his Savior, his Lord, and his God, he finds in Him all that he needs to answer the pressing question of sin and salvation, of life and death.

No one is excluded from this all-embracing "for your sakes." While extreme modern philosophy teaches the survival of the fittest and insists that the sick and the weak and the unproductive members of society be removed from the land of the living, here are the riches of Christ's invitation, "Come unto me, all ye that labour and are heavy laden." While India says of its baby girls, "Drown them!" and China echoes, "Sell them!" Jesus places His benediction upon childhood and says, *"Suffer the little children to come unto me, and forbid them not: for of such is the kingdom of God."* While Africa repudiates its aged and infirm and calls out, "Drag them out into the jungle!" and our modern system answers, "Over the hills to the poorhouse!" the riches of God's Word say, "And even to your old age I am he; and even to hoar hairs will I carry you." In short, never has man known any program that so completely obliterates every mark of human distinction as Christ's self-impoverization "for your sakes," that is, for the redemption of the world, in its absolute entirety.

The Magnificent Message to You

So tonight I invite you to come and to accept this magnificent promise of our text, "that ye through his poverty might be rich." I appeal directly and especially to those who have come from Christian homes and who have become untrue to the trust of God-fearing parents; to those who may have been members of the church of Jesus Christ but who permitted either the cares or the joys of this life to crowd out the feeling of their duties and responsibilities toward God; to those who may regard themselves beyond the pale of grace, who may feel that because of particular, repeated, and grievous sins in their own lives the grace and mercy of God does not extend to them. To all such, He, the unfailing Friend of sinners, has promised the inestimable riches that offer to the world today a happiness, a contentment, and a peace that passes all understanding. Have you been confronted by disillusionment and disappointment? Here in Christ's riches is the hope of the hopeless, the rock that stands firm and steadfast amid the flow and ebb of man's changing favors. Do you find yourself in the midst of inner struggles, in a surging conflict for which human resources grant no help? Here, in Christ's riches, you have Him who is the way and the truth and the life. Does your heart ache under the crushing pain of recent bereavement and the hurt that lies too deep to be probed by a physician's skill? Here, in Christ's riches, is the balm that soothes your sorrow and the radiance that guides you through the lowering darkness to the beacon of happiness, to Him that "doeth all things well." Are you anxiously striving to learn how to grow in sanctification, how to obtain the crown of life, how to gain the assurance of the blessed companionship with the Lord when life ends? Here is the goal of your search for here is Christ, who reaches out to you tonight to bestow upon all who will receive it the most magnificent gift in the world, His never-failing, never-ending grace.

Now, if there is some groping, questioning soul that interrupts, "How can I come?" "What does it cost?" "What must I do?" what an unparalleled privilege is mine to be able to tell such souls tonight not the opinion of human speculation but the positive truth of God's revelation to man: We are justified freely, by His grace, through the redemption that is in Christ Jesus, His Son! Christianity is the only free religion on the face of the earth. It must be free because there is not enough money in the world to compensate the price that the Lord Jesus paid for salvation. I read the other day of a manuscript of a child's story that was purchased for almost $150,000. Not long ago an automobile factory was sold for $146 million. Now, if men place such values upon the material things of life, what figures must be placed on the imperishable and everlasting grace of God? And yet, wonder of wonders, it is free! Not only need we pay nothing, but we need do nothing, for a lifetime of the most strenuous effort, intensify it as we may, could never accomplish the humanly impossible task of bringing men from earth to heaven.

Come, then, and take the vast resources of divine love that Christ holds out to you. Led on by rumors of fabulous wealth, men have strained every effort to uncover hidden treasures and to bring to light the unsealed riches of past ages. But here, in the time-defying, decay-challenging riches of the soul that Jesus offers through His abysmal poverty and limitless self-giving, your treasure of treasures is close at hand. Will you not come, then, tonight and take into grateful hearts the outpouring of this most magnificent gift that heaven has given to men? Will you not through trusting, childlike, implicit faith appropriate this unsearchable wealth of spirit for the enriching of your soul? Come, I beseech you, from sin to grace, from darkness to light, from poverty to riches, for Jesus' sake. Amen.

NOTES

The Doctrine of Election

John Calvin (1509–1564) has made his mark in history as a theologian and reformer, but he was preeminently a preacher of the Word. He ministered to the church in Geneva from 1541 to 1564, faithfully preaching the Scriptures and expounding God's truth. Weak in body and often afflicted with pain, he nevertheless kept to a disciplined program of study and was usually at his books by five or six in the morning. That great teacher of preachers, Dr. John Broadus, said that John Calvin "gave the ablest, soundest, clearest expositions of Scripture that had been seen in a thousand years."

This sermon is from *The Mystery of Godliness*, published in 1950 by Wm. B. Eerdmans, Grand Rapids.

John Calvin

4
THE DOCTRINE OF ELECTION

> Who hath saved us, and called us with an holy calling, not according to our works, but according to his own purpose and grace, which was given us in Christ Jesus before the world began, but is now made manifest by the appearing of our Saviour Jesus Christ, who hath abolished death, and hath brought life and immortality to light through the gospel (2 Timothy 1:9–10).

WE HAVE SHOWN this morning, according to the text of Saint Paul, that if we will know the free mercy of our God in saving us, we must come to His everlasting counsel whereby He chose us before the world began. For there we see He had no regard to our persons, neither to our worthiness nor to any deserts that we could possibly bring. Before we were born, we were enrolled in His register; He had already adopted us for His children. Therefore let us yield the whole to His mercy, knowing that we cannot boast of ourselves unless we rob Him of the honor that belongs to Him.

Men have endeavored to invent objections to darken the grace of God. For they have said, although God chose men before the world began, yet it was according as He foresaw that one would be diverse from another. The Scripture shows plainly that God did not wait to see whether men were worthy or not when He chose them. But the sophisters thought they might darken the grace of God by saying, though He regarded not the deserts that were past, He had an eye to those that were to come. For, say they, though Jacob and his brother Esau had done neither good nor evil, and God chose one and refused the other, yet notwithstanding He foresaw (as all things are present with Him) that Esau would be a vicious man and that Jacob would be as he afterward showed himself.

But these are foolish speculations, for they plainly make Saint Paul a liar, who says, God rendered no reward to our works when He chose us because He did it before the world began. But though the authority of Saint Paul were abolished, yet the matter is very plain and open not only in the Holy Scripture, but in reason, insomuch that those who would make an escape after this sort show themselves to be men void of all skill. For if we search ourselves to the bottom, what good can we find? Are not all mankind cursed? What do we bring from our mother's womb except sin?

Therefore we differ not one whit one from another. But it pleases God to take those to Himself whom He would. And for this cause Saint Paul uses these words in another place when he says, men have not whereof to rejoice, for no man finds himself better than his fellows, unless it be because God discerns him. So then, if we confess that God chose us before the world began, it necessarily follows that God prepared us to receive His grace; that He bestowed upon us that goodness which was not in us before; that He not only chose us to be heirs of the kingdom of heaven, but He likewise justifies us and governs us by His Holy Spirit. The Christian ought to be so well resolved in this doctrine that he is beyond doubt.

There are some men at this day that would be glad if the truth of God were destroyed. Such men fight against the Holy Spirit like mad beasts and endeavor to abolish the Holy Scripture. There is more honesty in the papists than in these men, for the doctrine of the papists is a great deal better, more holy, and more agreeable to the sacred Scripture than the doctrine of those vile and wicked men who cast down God's holy election—these dogs that bark at it and swine that root it up.

However, let us hold fast that which is here taught us: God having chosen us before the world had its course, we must attribute the cause of our salvation to His free goodness. We must confess that He did not take us to be His children for any deserts of our own, for we had nothing to recommend ourselves into His favor. Therefore, we must put the cause and fountain of our salvation in Him only and ground ourselves upon it. Otherwise, whatsoever and howsoever we build, it will come to nothing.

We must here notice what Saint Paul joins together, to wit, the grace of Jesus Christ with the everlasting counsel of God the Father, then he brings us to our calling that we may be assured of God's goodness and of His will that would have remained hid from us unless we had a witness of it. Saint Paul says in the first place that the grace that hangs upon the purpose of God and is comprehended in it is given in our Lord Jesus Christ, as if he said, seeing we deserve to be cast away and hated as God's mortal enemies, it was needful for us to be grafted, as it were, into Jesus Christ that God might acknowledge and allow us for His children. Otherwise, God could not look upon us, only hate us, because there is nothing but wretchedness in us. We are full of sin and stuffed up, as it were, with all kinds of iniquity.

God, who is justice itself, can have no agreement with us while He considers our sinful nature. Therefore, when He would adopt us before the world began, it was requisite that Jesus Christ should stand between us and Him, that we should be chosen in His person, for He is the well-beloved Son. When God joins us to Him, He makes us such as pleases Him. Let us learn to come directly to Jesus Christ if we will not doubt God's election, for He is the true looking glass wherein we must behold our adoption.

If Jesus Christ be taken from us, then is God a judge of sinners so that we cannot hope for any goodness or favor at His hands but look rather for vengeance. Without Jesus Christ, His majesty will always be terrible and fearful to us. If we hear mention made of His everlasting purpose, we cannot but be afraid as though He were already armed to plunge us into misery. But when we know that all grace rests in Jesus Christ, then we may be assured that God loved us, although we were unworthy.

In the second place, we must notice that Saint Paul speaks not simply of God's election, for that would not put us beyond doubt, but we should rather remain in perplexity and anguish. But he adds *the calling,* whereby God has opened His counsel that before was unknown to us and that we could not reach. How shall we know then that God has chosen us, that we may rejoice in Him and boast of the goodness that He has bestowed upon us? They that speak against God's election leave the Gospel alone. They leave all that God lays before us to bring us to Him, all the means that He has appointed for us and knows to be fit and proper for our use. We must not go on so, but according to Saint Paul's rule, we must join the calling with God's everlasting election.

It is said we are called; thus we have this second word, calling. Therefore God calls us. And how? surely, when it pleases Him to certify us of our election, which we could by no other means attain. For, as says the prophet Isaiah and also the apostle Paul, who can enter into God's counsel? But when it pleases God to communicate Himself to us familiarly, then we receive that which surmounts the knowledge of all men, for we have a good and faithful witness, which is the Holy Spirit, that raises us above the world and brings us even into the wonderful secrets of God.

We must not speak rashly of God's election and say, "We are predestinate." But if we will be thoroughly assured of our salvation, we must not speak lightly of it whether God has taken us to be His children or not. What then? Let us look at what is set forth in the Gospel. There God shows us that He is our Father. He will bring us to the inheritance of life, having marked us with the seal of the Holy Spirit in our hearts, which is an undoubted witness of our salvation if we receive it by faith.

The Gospel is preached to a great number that, notwithstanding, are reprobate. Yes, and God discovers and shows that He has cursed them, that they have no part nor portion in His kingdom because they resist the Gospel and cast away the grace that is offered them. But when we receive the doctrine of God with obedience and faith and rest ourselves upon His promises and accept this offer that He makes us to take us for His children, this, I say, is a certainty of our election. But we must here remark that when we have knowledge of our salvation, when God has called us and enlightened us in the faith of His Gospel, it is not to bring to nothing the everlasting predestination that went before.

There are a great many in these days that will say, who are they whom God has chosen but only the faithful? I grant it; but they make an evil consequence of it and say faith is the cause, yes, and the first cause of our salvation. If they called it a middle cause, it would indeed be true, for the Scripture says, "By grace are ye saved through faith" (Eph. 2:8). But we must go up higher, for if they attribute faith to men's free will, they blaspheme wickedly against God and commit sacrilege. We must come to that which the Scripture shows; to wit, when God gives us faith we must know that we are not capable of receiving the Gospel, only as He has framed us by the Holy Spirit.

It is not enough for us to hear the voice of man unless God work within and speak to us in a secret manner by the Holy Spirit, and from hence comes faith. But what is the cause of it? Why is faith given to one and not to another? Saint Luke shows us, saying, "As many as were ordained to eternal life believed" (Acts 13:48). There were a great number of hearers, and yet but few of them received the promise of salvation. And what few were they? those that were appointed to salvation. Again, Saint Paul speaks so largely upon this subject in his epistle to the Ephesians that it cannot be but the enemies of God's predestination are stupid and ignorant and that the Devil has plucked out their eyes and that they have become void of all reason if they cannot see a thing so plain and evident.

Saint Paul says, God has called us and made us partakers of His treasures and infinite riches which were given us through our Lord Jesus Christ, according as He had chosen us before the world began. When we say that we are called to salvation because God has given us faith, it is not because there is no higher cause. Whosoever cannot come to the everlasting election of God takes somewhat from Him and lessens His honor. This is found in almost every part of the Holy Scripture.

That we may make a short conclusion of this matter, let us see in what manner we ought to keep ourselves. When we inquire about our salvation, we must not begin to say, "Are we chosen?" No, we can never climb so high. We shall be confounded a thousand times and have our eyes dazzled before we can come to God's counsel. What then shall we do? Let us hear what is said in the Gospel. When God has been so gracious as to make us receive the promise offered, know we not that it is as much as if He had opened His whole heart to us and had registered our election in our consciences?

We must be certified that God has taken us for His children and that the kingdom of heaven is ours because we are called in Jesus Christ. How may we know this? How shall we stay ourselves upon the doctrine that God has set before us? We must magnify the grace of God and know that we can bring nothing to recommend ourselves to His favor. We must become nothing in our own eyes, that we may not claim any praise but know that God has called us to the Gospel, having chosen us before the world began. This election of God is, as it were, a sealed letter because it consists in itself and in its own nature. But we may read it, for God gives a witness of it when He calls us to Himself by the Gospel and by faith.

For even as the original or first copy takes nothing from the letter or writing that is read, even so must we be out of doubt of our salvation. When God certifies us by the Gospel that He takes us for His children, this testimony carries peace with it, being signed by the blood of our Lord Jesus Christ and sealed by the Holy Spirit. When we have this witness, have we not enough to content our minds? Therefore, God's election is so far from being against this that it confirms the witness that we have in the Gospel. We must not doubt but what God has registered our names before the world was made among His chosen children, but the knowledge thereof He reserved to Himself.

We must always come to our Lord Jesus Christ when we talk of our election, for without Him (as we have already shown), we cannot come near to God. When we talk of His decree, well may we be astonished as men worthy of death. But if Jesus Christ be our guide, we may with cheerfulness depend upon Him, knowing that He has worthiness enough in Him to make all His members beloved of God the Father. It is sufficient for us that we are grafted into His body and made one with Him. Thus we must muse upon this doctrine, if we will profit by it aright, as it is set forth by Saint Paul when he says this grace of salvation was given us *before the world began.* We must go beyond the order of nature if we will know how we are saved, and by what cause and from whence our salvation comes.

God would not leave us in doubt, neither would He hide His counsel that we might not know how our salvation was secured, but He has called us to Him by His Gospel and has sealed the witness of His goodness and fatherly love in our hearts. So then, having such a certainty, let us glorify God that He has called us of His free mercy. Let us rest ourselves upon our Lord Jesus Christ, knowing that He did not deceive us when He caused it to be preached that He gave Himself for us and witnessed it by the Holy Spirit. For faith is an undoubted token that God takes us for His children; thereby we are led to the everlasting election, according as He had chosen us before.

He says not that God has chosen us because we have heard the Gospel, but on the other hand, he attributes the faith that is given us to the highest cause to wit, because God has foreordained that He would save us, seeing we were lost and cast away in Adam. There are certain dolts who, to blind the eyes of the simple and such as are like themselves, say the grace of salvation was given us because God ordained that His Son should redeem mankind, and therefore this is common to all.

But Saint Paul spoke after another sort. Men cannot by such childish arguments mar the doctrine of the Gospel, for it is said plainly that God has saved us. Does this refer to all without exception? No; he speaks only of the faithful. Again, does Saint Paul include all the world? Some were called by preaching, and yet they made themselves unworthy of the salvation that was offered them; therefore they were reprobate. God left others in their unbelief who never heard the Gospel preached.

Therefore Saint Paul directed himself plainly and precisely to those whom God had chosen and reserved to Himself. God's goodness will never be viewed in its true light nor honored as it deserves unless we know that He would not have us remain in the general destruction of mankind, wherein He has left those that were like us, from whom we do not differ, for we are no better than they, but so it pleased God. Therefore all mouths must be stopped. Men must presume to take nothing upon themselves except to praise God, confessing themselves debtors to Him for all their salvation.

We shall now make some remarks upon the other words used by Saint Paul in this place. It is true that God's election could never be profitable to us, neither could it come to us unless we knew it by means of the Gospel. For this cause it pleased God to reveal that which He had kept secret before all ages. But to declare his meaning more plainly, he adds that this grace is revealed to us now. And how? "By the appearing of our Saviour Jesus Christ." When he says that this grace is revealed to us by the appearing of Jesus Christ, he shows that we should be too unthankful if we could not content and rest ourselves upon the grace of the Son of God. What can we look for more? If we could climb up beyond the clouds and search out the secrets of God, what would be the result of it? Would it not be to ascertain that we are His children and heirs?

Now we know these things, for they are clearly set forth in Jesus Christ. For it is said that all who believe in Him shall enjoy the privilege of being God's children. Therefore we must not swerve from these things one jot if we will be certified of our election. Saint Paul has already shown us that God never loved us nor chose us, only in the person of His beloved Son. When Jesus Christ appeared He revealed life to us, otherwise we should never have been the partakers of it. He has made us acquainted with the everlasting counsel of God. But it is presumption for men to attempt to know more than God would have them know.

If we walk soberly and reverently in obedience to God, hearing and receiving what He says in the Holy Scripture, the way will be made plain before us. Saint Paul says, when the Son of God appeared in the world, He opened our eyes that we might know that He was gracious to us before the world was made. We were received as His children and accounted just, so that we need not doubt but that the kingdom of heaven is prepared for us, not that we have it by our deserts but because it belongs to Jesus Christ, who makes us partakers with Himself.

When Saint Paul speaks of the appearing of Jesus Christ, he says, "He has brought life and immortality to light through the gospel." It is not only said that Jesus Christ is our Savior, but that He is sent to be a mediator to reconcile us by the sacrifice of His death. He is sent to us as a lamb without blemish, to purge us and make satisfaction for all our trespasses. He is our pledge, to deliver us from the condemnation of death. He is our righteousness; He is our advocate, who makes intercession with God that He would hear our prayers.

We must allow all these qualities to belong to Jesus Christ if we will know aright how He appeared. We must look at the substance contained in the Gospel. We must know that Jesus Christ appeared as our Savior and that He suffered for our salvation, that we were reconciled to God the Father through His means, that we have been cleansed from all our blemishes and freed from everlasting death. If we know not that He is our advocate, that He hears us when we pray to God to the end that our prayers may be answered, what will become of us? What confidence can we have to call upon God's name, who is the fountain of our salvation? But Saint Paul says, Jesus Christ has fulfilled all things that were requisite for the redemption of mankind.

If the Gospel were taken away, of what advantage would it be to us that the Son of God had suffered death and risen again the third day for our justification? All this would be unprofitable to us. So then, the Gospel puts us in possession of the benefits that Jesus Christ has purchased for us. And therefore, though He be absent from us in body and is not conversant with us here on earth, it is not that He has withdrawn Himself, as though we could not find Him. For the sun that shines does no more enlighten the world than Jesus Christ shows Himself openly to those that have the eyes of faith to look upon Him when the Gospel is preached. Therefore Saint Paul says, Jesus Christ has brought *life to light*, yes, everlasting life.

He says, the Son of God has abolished death. And how did He abolish it? If He had not offered an everlasting sacrifice to appease the wrath of God, if He had not entered even to the bottomless pit to draw us from thence, if He had not taken our curse upon Himself, if He had not taken away the burden wherewith we were crushed down, where should we have been? Would death have been destroyed? No, sin would reign in us, and death, likewise. And indeed, let everyone examine himself, and we shall find that we are slaves to Satan, who is the prince of death, so that we are shut up in this miserable slavery, unless God destroy the Devil, sin, and death. And this is done. But how? He has taken away our sins by the blood of our Lord Jesus Christ.

Therefore, though we be poor sinners and in danger of God's judgment, yet sin cannot hurt us. The sting, which is venomous, is so blunted that it cannot wound us because Jesus Christ has gained the victory over it.

He suffered not the shedding of His blood in vain. But it was a washing wherewith we were washed through the Holy Spirit, as is shown by Saint Peter. And thus we see plainly that when Saint Paul speaks of the Gospel, wherein Jesus Christ appeared and appears daily to us, he forgets not His death and passion nor the things that pertain to the salvation of mankind.

We may be certified that in the person of our Lord Jesus Christ we have all that we can desire. We have full and perfect trust in the goodness of God and the love He bears us. We see that our sins separate us from God and cause a warfare in our members, yet we have an atonement through our Lord Jesus Christ. And why so? Because He has shed His blood to wash away our sins. He has offered a sacrifice whereby God has become reconciled to us. To be short, He has taken away the curse that we may be blessed of God. Moreover, He has conquered death and triumphed over it that He might deliver us from the tyranny thereof, which otherwise would entirely overwhelm us.

Thus we see that all things that belong to our salvation are accomplished in our Lord Jesus Christ. And that we may enter into full possession of all these benefits, we most know that He appears to us daily by His Gospel. Although He dwells in His heavenly glory, if we open the eyes of our faith we shall behold Him. We must learn not to separate that which the Holy Spirit has joined together. Let us observe what Saint Paul meant by a comparison to amplify the grace that God showed to the world after the coming of our Lord Jesus Christ, as if he said, the old fathers had not this advantage to have Jesus Christ appear to them as He appeared to us.

It is true, they had the self-same faith, and the inheritance of heaven is theirs as well as ours, God having revealed His grace to them as well as us, but not in like measure, for they saw Jesus Christ afar off under the figures of the law, as Saint Paul says to the Corinthians. The veil of the temple was as yet stretched out that the Jews could not come near the sanctuary, that is, the material sanctuary. But now, the veil of the temple having been removed, we draw near to the majesty of our God. We come most familiarly to Him in whom dwells all perfection and glory. In short, we have the body, whereas they had but the shadow (Col. 2:17).

The ancient Fathers submitted themselves wholly to bear the affliction of Jesus Christ, as it is said in the eleventh chapter of the Hebrews. For it is not said Moses bore the shame of Abraham, but of Jesus Christ. Thus the ancient Fathers, though they lived under the law, offered themselves to God in sacrifices to bear most patiently the afflictions of Christ. And now Jesus Christ, having risen from the dead, has brought *life to light*. If we are so delicate that we cannot bear the afflictions of the Gospel, are we not worthy to be blotted from the book of God and cast off? Therefore, we must be constant in the faith and ready to suffer for the name of Jesus Christ, whatsoever God will, because life is set before us, and we have a more familiar knowledge of it than the ancient Fathers had.

We know how the ancient Fathers were tormented by tyrants and enemies of the truth and how they suffered constantly. The condition of the church is not more grievous in these days than it was then. For now has Jesus Christ brought life and immortality to light through the Gospel. As often as the grace of God is preached to us, it is as much as if the kingdom of heaven were opened to us, as if God reached out His hand and certified us that life is near and that He will make us partakers of His heavenly inheritance. But when we look to this life that was purchased for us by our Lord Jesus Christ, we should not hesitate to forsake all that we have in this world to come to the treasure above, which is in heaven.

Therefore, let us not be willingly blind, seeing Jesus Christ lays daily before us the life and immortality spoken of here. When Saint Paul speaks of life and adds immortality, it is as much as if he said, we already enter into the kingdom of heaven by faith. Though we be as strangers here below, the life and grace of which we are made partakers through our Lord Jesus Christ shall bring its fruit in convenient time, to wit, when He shall be sent of God the Father to show us the effect of things that are daily preached which were fulfilled in His person when He was clad in humanity.

Great Guilt No Obstacle to the Pardon of the Returning Sinner

Jonathan Edwards (1703–1758) was a Congregational preacher, a theologian, and a philosopher, possessing one of the greatest minds ever produced on the American continent. He graduated with highest honors from Yale in 1720, and in 1726 was ordained and served as co-pastor with his grandfather, Solomon Stoddard, in Northfield, Massachusetts. When Stoddard died in 1729, Edwards became sole pastor, a position he held until doctrinal disagreements with the church led to his resignation in 1750. He played a key role in the Great Awakening (1734–44) and is perhaps best known for his sermon "Sinners in the Hands of an Angry God."

This sermon is taken from *The Works of Jonathan Edwards,* volume 2, published by Banner of Truth Trust in 1976.

Jonathan Edwards

5

GREAT GUILT NO OBSTACLE TO THE PARDON OF THE RETURNING SINNER

For thy name's sake, O LORD, pardon mine iniquity; for it is great (Psalm 25:11).

IT IS EVIDENT by some passages in this psalm that when it was penned it was a time of affliction and danger with David. This appears particularly by the fifteenth and following verses: "Mine eyes are ever toward the LORD; for he shall pluck my feet out of the net." His distress makes him think of his sins and leads him to confess them and to cry to God for pardon, as is suitable in a time of affliction. "Remember not the sins of my youth, nor my transgressions" (v. 7); and, "Look upon mine affliction and my pain; and forgive all my sins" (v. 18).

It is observable in the text what arguments the psalmist makes use of in pleading for pardon.

1. He pleads for pardon *for God's name's sake*. He has no expectation of pardon for the sake of any righteousness or worthiness of his for any good deeds he had done or any compensation he had made for his sins. If man's righteousness could be a just plea, David would have had as much to plead as most. But he begs that God would do it for His own name's sake, for His own glory, for the glory of His own free grace, and for the honor of His own covenant-faithfulness.

2. The psalmist pleads *the greatness of his sins* as an argument for mercy. He does not plead his own righteousness or the smallness of his sins. He does not say, Pardon mine iniquity, for I have done much good to counterbalance it; or, Pardon mine iniquity, for it is

small and You have no great reason to be angry with me. Mine iniquity is not so great that You have any just cause to remember it against me. Mine offense is not such but that You may well enough overlook it. But on the contrary he says, "Pardon mine iniquity; for it is great." He pleads the greatness of his sin and not the smallness of it. He enforces his prayer with this consideration, that his sins are very heinous.

But how could he make this a plea for pardon? I answer, because the greater his iniquity was, the more need he had of pardon. It is as much as if he had said, "Pardon mine iniquity, for it is so great that I cannot bear the punishment. My sin is so great that I am in necessity of pardon. My case will be exceedingly miserable unless You be pleased to pardon me." He makes use of the greatness of his sin to enforce his plea for pardon as a man would make use of the greatness of calamity in begging for relief. When a beggar begs for bread, he will plead the greatness of his poverty and necessity. When a man in distress cries for pity, what more suitable plea can be urged than the extremity of his case? And God allows such a plea as this, for He is moved to mercy toward us by nothing in us but the miserableness of our case. He does not pity sinners because they are worthy but because they need His pity.

Doctrine

If we truly come to God for mercy, the greatness of our sin will no impediment to pardon. If it were an impediment, David would never have used it as a plea for pardon, as we find he does in the text. The following things are needful in order that we truly come to God for mercy.

We should see our misery, and be sensible of our need of mercy. They who are not sensible of their misery cannot truly look to God for mercy, for it is the very notion of divine mercy that it is the goodness and grace of God to the miserable. Without misery in the object, there can be no exercise of mercy. To suppose mercy without supposing misery, or pity without calamity, is a contradiction. Therefore men cannot look upon themselves as proper objects of mercy unless they first know themselves to be miserable, and so unless this be the case, it is impossible that they should come to God for mercy. They must be sensible that they are the children of wrath, that the law is against them, that they are exposed to the curse of it, that the wrath of God abides on them, and that He is angry with them every day while they are under the guilt of sin. They must be sensible that it is a very dreadful thing to be the object of the wrath of God, that it is a very awful thing to have Him for their enemy, and that they cannot bear His wrath. They must be sensible that the guilt of sin makes them miserable creatures, whatever temporal enjoyments they have; that they can be no other than miserable, undone creatures so long as God is angry with them; that they are without strength and must perish, and that eternally, unless God helps them. They must see that their case is utterly desperate for anything that anyone else can do for them, that they hang over the pit of eternal misery, and that they must necessarily drop into it if God have not mercy on them.

We must be sensible that we are not worthy that God should have mercy on us. They who truly come to God for mercy come as beggars and not as creditors. They come for mere mercy, for sovereign grace, and not for anything that is due. Therefore, they must see that the misery under which they lie is justly brought upon them, and that the wrath to which they are exposed is justly threatened against them. They have deserved that God should be their enemy, and should continue to be their enemy. They must be sensible that it would be just with God to do as He has threatened in His holy law—make them the objects of His wrath and curse, in hell to all eternity. They who come to God for mercy in a right manner are not disposed to find fault with His severity. But they come in a sense of their own utter unworthiness, as with ropes about their necks and lying in the dust at the foot of mercy.

We must come to God for mercy in and through Jesus Christ alone. All our hope of mercy must be from the consideration of what He is, what He has done, and what He has suffered. There is no other name under heaven, given among men, whereby we can be saved but that of Christ. He is the Son of God and the Savior of the world. His blood cleanses from all sin, and He is so worthy that all sinners who are in Him may well be pardoned and accepted. It is impossible that any should come to God for mercy, and at the same time have no hope of mercy. Their coming to God for it implies that they have some hope of obtaining, otherwise they would not think it worth the while to come. But they that come in a right manner have all their hope through Christ, from the consideration of His redemption and the sufficiency of it. If persons thus come to God for mercy, the greatness of their sins will be no impediment to pardon. Let their sins be ever so many and great and aggravated, it will not make God in the least degree more backward to pardon them. This may be made evident by the following considerations.

1. The mercy of God is as sufficient for the pardon of the greatest sins as for the least because His mercy is infinite. That which is infinite is as much above what is great as it is above what is small. Thus, God being infinitely great, He is as much above kings as He is above beggars; He is as much above the highest angel as He is above the meanest worm. One infinite measure does not come any nearer to the extent of what is infinite than another. So the mercy of God being infinite, it must be as sufficient for the pardon of all sin as of one. If one of the least sins be not beyond the mercy of God, so neither are the greatest, or ten thousand of them. However, it must be acknowledged that this alone does not prove the doctrine. For though the mercy of God may be as sufficient for the pardon of great sins as others, yet there may be other obstacles besides the want of mercy. The mercy of God may be sufficient, and yet the other attributes may oppose the dispensation of mercy in these cases.

2. Therefore, I observe that the satisfaction of Christ is as sufficient for the removal of the greatest guilt as the least: The blood of Christ cleanseth from all sin (1 John 1:7). "By him all that believe are justified from all things, from which ye could not be justified by the law of Moses" (Acts 13:39). All the sins of those who truly come to God for mercy, let them be what they will, are satisfied, for God is true who tells us so. If they be satisfied, surely it is not incredible that God should be ready to pardon them. So that Christ having fully satisfied for all sin, or having wrought out a satisfaction that is sufficient for all, is now in no way inconsistent with the glory of the divine attributes to pardon the greatest sins of those who in a right manner come to Him for it. God may now pardon the greatest sinners without any prejudice to the honor of His holiness. The holiness of God will not suffer Him to give the least countenance to sin but inclines Him to give proper testimonies of His hatred of it. But Christ having satisfied for sin, God can now love the sinner and give no countenance at all to sin however great a sinner he may have been. It was a sufficient testimony of God's abhorrence of sin that He poured out His wrath on His own dear Son when He took the guilt of it in upon Himself. Nothing can more show God's abhorrence of sin than this. If all mankind had been eternally damned, it would not have been so great a testimony of it.

3. God may, through Christ, pardon the greatest sinner without any prejudice to the honor of His majesty. The honor of the divine majesty indeed requires satisfaction, but the sufferings of Christ fully repair the injury. Let the contempt be ever so great, yet if so honorable a person as Christ undertakes to be a mediator for the offender and suffers so much for him, it fully repairs the injury done to the Majesty of heaven and earth. The sufferings of Christ fully satisfy justice. The justice of God as the supreme governor and judge of the world requires the punishment of sin. The supreme judge must judge the world according to a rule

of justice. God does not show mercy as a judge but as a sovereign; therefore His exercise of mercy as a sovereign, and His justice as a judge must be made consistent one with another. This is done by the sufferings of Christ, in which sin is punished fully and justice answered. "Whom God hath set forth to be a propitiation through faith in his blood, to declare his righteousness for the remission of sins that are past, through the forbearance of God; to declare, I say, at this time, his righteousness: that he might be just, and the justifier of him which believeth in Jesus." The law is no impediment in the way of the pardon of the greatest sin if men do but truly come to God for mercy, for Christ has fulfilled the law; He has borne the curse of it in His sufferings. "Christ hath redeemed us from the curse of the law, being made a curse for us: for it is written, Cursed is every one that hangeth on a tree."

4. Christ will not refuse to save the greatest sinners who in a right manner come to God for mercy, for this is His work. It is His business to be a Savior of sinners. It is the work upon which He came into the world; therefore, He will not object to it. He did not come to call the righteous, but sinners, to repentance (see Matt. 9:13). Sin is the very evil which He came into the world to remedy. Therefore He will not object to any man that he is very sinful. The more sinful he is, the more need of Christ. The sinfulness of man was the reason of Christ's coming into the world. This is the very misery from which He came to deliver men. The more they have of it, the more need they have of being delivered: "They that be whole need not a physician, but they that are sick" (Matt. 9:12). The physician will not make it an objection against healing a man who applies to him, that he stands in great need of his help. If a physician of compassion comes among the sick and wounded, surely he will not refuse to heal those that stand in most need of healing, if he be able to heal them.

5. Herein does the glory of grace by the redemption of Christ much consist in its sufficiency for the pardon

of the greatest sinners. The whole contrivance of the way of salvation is for this end, to glorify the free grace of God. God had it on His heart from all eternity to glorify this attribute; therefore it is that the device of saving sinners by Christ was conceived. The greatness of divine grace appears very much in this, that God by Christ saves the greatest offenders. The greater the guilt of any sinner is, the more glorious and wonderful is the grace manifested in his pardon: "Where sin abounded, grace did much more abound" (Rom. 5:20). The apostle, when telling how great a sinner he had been, takes notice of the abounding of grace in his pardon, of which his great guilt was the occasion: "Who was before a blasphemer, and a persecutor, and injurious. But I obtained mercy. . . . And the grace of our Lord was exceeding abundant with faith and love which is in Christ Jesus" (1 Tim. 1:13–14). The Redeemer is glorified in that He proves sufficient to redeem those who are exceeding sinful, in that His blood proves sufficient to wash away the greatest guilt, in that He is able to save men to the uttermost, and in that He redeems even from the greatest misery. It is the honor of Christ to save the greatest sinners when they come to Him, as it is the honor of a physician that he cures the most desperate diseases or wounds. Therefore, no doubt, Christ will be willing to save the greatest sinners if they come to Him, for He will not be backward to glorify Himself and to commend the value and virtue of His own blood. Seeing He has so laid out Himself to redeem sinners, He will not be unwilling to show that He is able to redeem to the uttermost.

6. Pardon is as much offered and promised to the greatest sinners as any, if they will come aright to God for mercy. The invitations of the Gospel are always in universal terms: Ho, *every one* that thirsteth; come unto me, *all ye* that labour and are heavy laden; and, *whosoever* will, let him come. And the voice of wisdom is to men in general: "Unto you, O men, I call; and my voice is to the sons of men" (Prov. 8:4)—not to moral men, or religious men, but *to you, O men.* So Christ

promises: "Him that cometh to me I will in no wise cast out" (John 6:37). This is the direction of Christ to His apostles after His resurrection: "Go ye into all the world, and preach the gospel to every creature. He that believeth and is baptized shall be saved" (Mark 16:15–16). Which is agreeable to what the apostle saith, that the gospel" was preached to every creature which is under heaven" (Col. 1:23).

Application

The proper use of this subject is to encourage sinners whose consciences are burdened with a sense of guilt immediately to go to God through Christ for mercy. If you go in the manner we have described, the arms of mercy are open to embrace you. You need not be at all the more fearful of coming because of your sins, let them be ever so black. If you had as much guilt lying on each of your souls as all the wicked men in the world and all the damned souls in hell, yet if you come to God for mercy, sensible of your own vileness and seeking pardon only through the free mercy of God in Christ, you would not need to be afraid. The greatness of your sins would be no impediment to your pardon. Therefore, if your souls be burdened and you are distressed for fear of hell, you need not bear that burden and distress any longer. If you are but willing, you may freely come and unload yourselves and cast all your burdens on Christ and rest in Him.

But here I shall speak to some objections that some awakened sinners may be ready to make against what I now exhort them to.

I have spent my youth and all the best of my life in sin, and I am afraid God will not accept me when I offer Him only mine old age.

1. Has God said anywhere that He will not accept old sinners who come to Him? God has often made offers and promises in universal terms. Is there any such exception put in? Does Christ say, All that thirst, let them come to me and drink—except old sinners? Come to me, all ye that labor and are heavy laden—

except old sinners—and I will give you rest? Him that comes to me, I will in no wise cast out—if he be not an old sinner? Did you ever read any such exception anywhere in the Bible? And why should you give way to exceptions that you make out of your own heads or rather, that the Devil puts into your heads and that have no foundation in the Word of God? Indeed it is more rare that old sinners are willing to come than others; but if they do come, they are as readily accepted as any whatever.

2. When God accepts of young persons, it is not for the sake of the service that they are likely to do for Him afterward or because youth is better worth accepting than old age. You seem entirely to mistake the matter in thinking that God will not accept you because you are old, as though He readily accepted of persons in their youth because their youth is better worth His acceptance, whereas it is only for the sake of Jesus Christ that God is willing to accept any.

You say your life is almost spent, and you are afraid that the best time for serving God is past. Therefore God will not now accept you, as if it were for the sake of the service that persons are like to do for Him after they are converted that He accepts them. But a self-righteous spirit is at the bottom of such objections. Men cannot get off from the notion that it is for some goodness or service of their own, either done or expected to be done, that God accepts persons and receives them into favor. Indeed they who deny God their youth, the best part of their lives, and spend it in the service of Satan dreadfully sin and provoke God; He very often leaves them to hardness of heart when they are grown old. But if they are willing to accept of Christ when old, He is as ready to receive them as any others. For in that matter God has respect only to Christ and His worthiness.

But I am afraid that I have committed sins that are peculiar to reprobates. I have sinned against light and strong convictions of conscience. I have sinned presumptuously and have so resisted the strivings of the

Spirit of God that I am afraid I have committed such sins as none of God's elect ever commit. I cannot think that God will ever leave one whom He intends to save to go on and commit sins against so much light and conviction and with such horrid presumption. Others may say, I have had risings of heart against God—blasphemous thoughts, a spiteful and malicious spirit. I have abused mercy and the strivings of the Spirit, trampled upon the Savior, and my sins are such as are peculiar to those who are reprobated to eternal damnation.

1. There is no sin peculiar to reprobates but the sin against the Holy Spirit. Do you read of any other in the Word of God? And if you do not read of any there, what ground have you to think any such thing? What other rule have we by which to judge of such matters but the divine Word? If we venture to go beyond that, we shall be miserably in the dark. When we pretend to go further in our determinations than the Word of God, Satan takes us up and leads us. It seems to you that such sins are peculiar to the reprobate and such as God never forgives. But what reason can you give for it if you have no Word of God to reveal it? Is it because you cannot see how the mercy of God is sufficient to pardon or the blood of Christ to cleanse from such presumptuous sins? If so, it is because you never yet saw how great the mercy of God is; you never saw the sufficiency of the blood of Christ, and you know not how far the virtue of it extends. Some elect persons have been guilty of all manner of sins, except the sin against the Holy Spirit. Unless you have been guilty of this, you have not been guilty of any that are peculiar to reprobates.

2. Men may be less likely to believe for sins that they have committed and not the less readily pardoned when they do believe. It must be acknowledged that some sinners are in more danger of hell than others. Though all are in great danger, some are less likely to be saved. Some are less likely ever to be converted and to come to Christ, but all who do come to Him are alike readily accepted. There is as much encouragement for one man to come to Christ as another. Such sins as

you mention are indeed exceedingly heinous and provoking to God and do in an especial manner bring the soul into danger of damnation and into danger of being given to final hardness of heart. God more commonly gives men up to the judgment of final hardness for such sins than for others. Yet they are not peculiar to reprobates. There is but one sin that is so—that against the Holy Spirit. And notwithstanding the sins that you have committed, if you can find it in your hearts to come to Christ and close with Him, you will be accepted not at all the less readily because you have committed such sins. Though God does more rarely cause some sorts of sinners to come to Christ than others, it is not because His mercy or the redemption of Christ is not as sufficient for them as others, but because in wisdom He sees fit so to dispense His grace for a restraint upon the wickedness of men, because it is His will to give converting grace in the use of means, among which this is one, to lead a moral and religious life, and agreeable to our light and the convictions of our consciences. But when once any sinner is willing to come to Christ, mercy is as ready for him as for any. There is no consideration at all of his sins. Let him have been ever so sinful, his sins are not remembered. God does not upbraid him with them.

But had I not better stay until I shall have made myself better before I presume to come to Christ? I have been, and see myself to be, very wicked now but am in hopes of mending myself and rendering myself at least not so wicked. Then I shall have more courage to come to God for mercy.

1. Consider how unreasonably you act. You are striving to set up yourselves for your own saviors; you are striving to get something of your own on the account of which you may the more readily be accepted, so that by this it appears that you do not seek to be accepted only on Christ's account. And is not this to rob Christ of the glory of being your only Savior? Yet this is the way in which you are hoping to make Christ willing to save you.

You can never come to Christ at all unless you first see that He will not accept you any more readily for anything that you can do. You must first see that it is utterly in vain for you to try to make yourselves better on any such account. You must see that you can never make yourselves any more worthy, or less unworthy, by anything that you can perform.

2. If ever you truly come to Christ, you must see that there is enough in Him for your pardon, though you be no better than you are. If you see not the sufficiency of Christ to pardon you, without any righteousness of your own to recommend you, you never will come so as to be accepted of Him. The way to be accepted is to come—not on any such encouragement that now you have made yourselves better and more worthy, or not so unworthy, but on the mere encouragement of Christ's worthiness and God's mercy.

3. If ever you truly come to Christ, you must come to Him to make you better. You must come as a patient comes to his physician with his diseases or wounds to be cured. Spread all your wickedness before Him and do not plead your goodness; plead your badness and your necessity on that account. Say, as the psalmist in the text, not, Pardon mine iniquity, for it is not so great as it was; but, "Pardon mine iniquity, for it is great."

NOTES

The Method of Grace

George Whitefield (1714–1770) was born in Gloucester, England, and educated at Pembroke College, Oxford. There he came under the influence of John Wesley and Charles Wesley, although Whitefield was more Calvinistic in doctrine than they. Ordained in the Anglican Church, he quickly gained a reputation as an effective preacher, but the Anglican churches disapproved of him because of his association with the Methodists. He began to preach to great crowds out of doors and led John Wesley to follow his example. Whitefield made seven visits to America and is recognized as one of the leaders of evangelism and spiritual awakening in American history.

This sermon is taken from *Select Sermons of George Whitefield,* published by Banner of Truth Trust.

George Whitefield

6
THE METHOD OF GRACE

> They have healed also the hurt of the daughter of my people slightly, saying, Peace, peace; when there is no peace (Jeremiah 6:14).

As GOD CAN send a nation or people no greater blessing than to give them faithful, sincere, and upright ministers, so the greatest curse that God can possibly send upon a people in this world is to give them over to blind, unregenerate, carnal, lukewarm, and unskilled guides. And yet, in all ages, we find that there have been many wolves in sheep's clothing, many that daubed with untempered mortar, that prophesied smoother things than God did allow. As it was formerly, so it is now; there are many that corrupt the Word of God and deal deceitfully with it.

It was so in a special manner in the prophet Jeremiah's time. He, faithful to his Lord, faithful to that God who employed him, did not fail from time to time to open his mouth against them and to bear a noble testimony to the honor of that God in whose name he from time to time spoke. If you will read his prophecy, you will find that none spoke more against such ministers than Jeremiah, and here especially in the chapter out of which the text is taken, he speaks very severely against them. He charges them with several crimes; particularly, he charges them with covetousness: "For," says he in the thirteenth verse, "from the least of them even unto the greatest of them every one is given to covetousness; and from the prophet even unto the priest every one dealeth falsely." And then, in the words of the text, in a more special manner, he exemplifies how they had dealt falsely, how they had behaved treacherously to poor souls. Says he, "They have healed also the hurt of the daughter of my people slightly, saying, Peace, peace; when there is no peace."

The prophet, in the name of God, had been denouncing war against the people. He had been telling them that their house should be left desolate and that the Lord would certainly visit the land with war. "Therefore," says he, in verses 11 and 12,

> I am full of the fury of the LORD; I am weary with holding in: I will pour it out upon the children abroad, and upon the assembly of young men together: for even the husband with the wife shall be taken, the aged with him that is full of days. And their houses shall be turned unto others, with their fields and wives together: for I will stretch out my hand upon the inhabitants of the land, saith the LORD.

The prophet gives a thundering message that they might be terrified and have some convictions and inclinations to repent. But it seems that the false prophets, the false priests, went about stifling people's convictions. When they were hurt or a little terrified, they were for daubing over the wound, telling them that Jeremiah was but an enthusiastic preacher, that there could be no such thing as war among them, and saying to people, Peace, peace, be still, when the prophet told them there was no peace.

The words, then, refer primarily to outward things but I verily believe have also a further reference to the soul and are to be referred to those false teachers who, when people were under conviction of sin, when people were beginning to look toward heaven, were for stifling their convictions and telling them they were good enough before. And, indeed, people generally love to have it so. Our hearts are exceedingly deceitful and desperately wicked; none but the eternal God knows how treacherous they are. How many of us cry, Peace, peace, to our souls, when there is no peace! How many are there who are now settled upon their lees, that now think they are Christians, that now flatter themselves that they have an interest in Jesus Christ, whereas if we come to examine their experiences, we shall find that their peace is but a peace of the Devil's making. It is not a peace of God's giving; it is not a peace that passes human understanding.

It is matter, therefore, of great importance, my dear hearers, to know whether we may speak peace to our hearts. We are all desirous of peace; peace is an unspeakable blessing. How can we live without peace? And, therefore, people from time to time must be taught how far they must go and what must be wrought in them before they can speak peace to their hearts. This is what I design at present, that I may deliver my soul, that I may be free from the blood of those to whom I preach, that I may not fail to declare the whole counsel of God. I shall, from the words of the text, endeavor to show you what you must undergo and what must be wrought in you before you can speak peace to your hearts.

But before I come directly to this, give me leave to premise a caution or two. And the first is, that I take it for granted you believe religion to be an inward thing. You believe it to be a work in the heart, a work wrought in the soul by the power of the Spirit of God. If you do not believe this, you do not believe your Bibles. If you do not believe this, though you have your Bibles in your hands, you hate the Lord Jesus Christ in your hearts. For religion is everywhere represented in Scripture as the work of God in the heart. The kingdom of God is within us, says our Lord; and, He is not a Christian who is one outwardly; but he is a Christian who is one inwardly. If any of you place religion in outward things, I shall not perhaps please you this morning. You will understand me no more when I speak of the work of God upon a poor sinner's heart than if I were talking in an unknown tongue.

I would further premise a caution that I would by no means confine God to one way of acting. I would by no means say that all persons, before they come to have a settled peace in their hearts, are obliged to undergo the same degrees of conviction. No; God has various ways of bringing His children home. His sacred Spirit blows when and where and how it listeth. But, however, I will venture to affirm this, that before ever you can speak peace to your hearts, whether by shorter or longer continuance of your convictions, whether in a more pungent or in a more gentle way, you must undergo what I shall hereafter lay down in the following discourse.

First, then, before you can speak peace to your hearts, you must be made to see, made to feel, made to weep over, made to bewail, your actual transgressions against the law of God. According to the covenant of works, "The soul that sinneth, it shall die"; cursed is that man, be he what he may, that continues not in all things that are written in the book of the law to do them. We are not only to do some things, but we are to do all things. We are to continue so to do, so that the least deviation from the moral law, according to the covenant of works, whether in thought, word, or deed, deserves eternal death at the hand of God. And if one evil thought, if one evil word, if one evil action, deserves eternal damnation, how many hells, my friends, do every one of us deserve, whose whole lives have been one continued rebellion against God! Before ever, therefore, you can speak peace to your hearts, you must be brought to see, brought to believe, what a dreadful thing it is to depart from the living God.

And now, my dear friends, examine your hearts, for I hope you came hither with a design to have your souls made better. Give me leave to ask you, in the presence of God, whether you know the time, and if you do not know exactly the time, do you know there was a time when God wrote bitter things against you, when the arrows of the Almighty were within you? Was ever the remembrance of your sins grievous to you? Was the burden of your sins intolerable to your thoughts? Did you ever see that God's wrath might justly fall upon you on account of your actual transgressions against God? Were you ever in all your life sorry for your sins? Could you ever say, My sins

Whitefield: *The Method of Grace* / 81

are gone over my head as a burden too heavy for me to bear? Did you ever experience any such thing as this? Did ever any such thing as this pass between God and your soul? If not, for Jesus Christ's sake, do not call yourselves Christians; you may speak peace to your hearts, but there is no peace. May the Lord awaken you, may the Lord convert you, may the Lord give you peace, if it be His will, before you go home!

But further: you may be convinced of your actual sins, so as to be made to tremble, and yet you may be strangers to Jesus Christ. You may have no true work of grace upon your hearts. Before ever, therefore, you can speak peace to your hearts, conviction must go deeper. You must not only be convinced of your actual transgressions against the law of God, but likewise of the foundation of all your transgressions. And what is that? I mean original sin, that original corruption each of us brings into the world with us, which renders us liable to God's wrath and damnation.

There are many poor souls that think themselves fine reasoners, yet they pretend to say there is no such thing as original sin. They will charge God with injustice in imputing Adam's sin to us; although we have the mark of the beast and of the Devil upon us, yet they tell us we are not born in sin. Let them look abroad into the world and see the disorders in it and think, if they can, if this is the paradise in which God did put man. No! Everything in the world is out of order. I have often thought, when I was abroad, that if there were no other argument to prove original sin, the rising of wolves and tigers against man, no, the barking of a dog against us, is a proof of original sin. Tigers and lions would not rise against us if it were not for Adam's first sin. For when the creatures rise up against us, it is as much as to say, You have sinned against God, and we take up our Master's quarrel. If we look inwardly, we shall see enough of lusts and man's temper contrary to the temper of God. There is pride, malice, and revenge in all our hearts. This temper cannot come from God; it comes from our first parent, Adam, who, after he fell from God, fell out of God into the Devil. However some people may deny this, yet when conviction comes, all carnal reasonings are battered down immediately, and the poor soul begins to feel and see the fountain from which all the polluted streams do flow.

When the sinner is first awakened, he begins to wonder, How came I to be so wicked? The Spirit of God then strikes in and shows that he has no good thing in him by nature. Then he sees that he is altogether gone out of the way, that he is altogether become abominable, and the poor creature is made to lie down at the foot of the throne of God and to acknowledge that God would be just to damn him, just to cut him off, though he never had committed one actual sin in his life. Did you ever feel and experience this, any of you—to justify God in your damnation—to own that you are by nature children of wrath and that God may justly cut you off, though you never actually had offended Him in all your life? If you were ever truly convicted, if your hearts were ever truly cut, if self were truly taken out of you, you would be made to see and feel this.

And if you have never felt the weight of original sin, do not call yourselves Christians. I am verily persuaded original sin is the greatest burden of a true convert; this ever grieves the regenerate soul, the sanctified soul. The indwelling of sin in the heart is the burden of a converted person; it is the burden of a true Christian. He continually cries out, "O. . . ! who shall deliver me from the body of this death?" this indwelling corruption in my heart? This is that which disturbs a poor soul most. And, therefore, if you never felt this inward corruption, if you never saw that God might justly curse you for it, indeed, my dear friends, you may speak peace to your hearts, but I fear—no—I know, there is no true peace.

Further: before you can speak peace to your hearts, you must not only be troubled for the sins of your life, the sin of your nature, but likewise for the sins of your best duties and performances. When a poor soul is somewhat awakened by the terrors of the Lord, then the poor creature, being born under the covenant of works, flies directly to a covenant of works again. And as Adam and Eve hid themselves among the trees of the garden and sewed fig leaves together to cover their nakedness, so the poor sinner, when awakened, flies to his duties and to his performances to hide himself from God and goes to patch up a righteousness of his own. Says he, I will be mighty good now—I will reform—I will do all I can; then certainly Jesus Christ will have mercy on me. But before you can speak peace to your heart, you must be brought to see that God may damn you for the best prayer you ever put up. You must be brought to see that all your duties, all your righteousness—as the prophet elegantly expresses it—put them all together, are so far from recommending you to God, are so far from being any motive and inducement to God to have mercy on your poor soul that He will see them to be filthy rags, a menstruous cloth that God hates, if you bring them to Him in order to recommend you to His favor.

My dear friends, what is there in our performances to recommend us to God? Our persons are in an unjustified state by nature, we deserve to be damned ten thousand times over, and what must our performances be? We can do no good thing by nature: "They that are in the flesh cannot please God." You may do things materially good, but you cannot do a thing formally and rightly good because nature cannot act above itself. It is impossible that a man who is unconverted can act for the glory of God; he cannot do anything in faith, and "whatsoever is not of faith is sin." After we are renewed, yet we are renewed but in part; indwelling sin continues in us. There is a mixture of corruption in every one of our duties, so that after we are converted, were Jesus Christ only to accept us according to our works, our works would damn us, for we cannot put up a prayer but it is far from that perfection which the moral law requires. I do not know what you may think, but I can say that I cannot pray but I sin—I cannot preach to you or any others but I sin—I can do nothing without sin. As one expresses it, my repentance wants to be repented of, and my tears to be washed in the precious blood of my dear Redeemer.

Our best duties are as so many splendid sins. Before you can speak peace in your heart, you must not only be made sick of your original and actual sin, but you must be made sick of your righteousness, of all your duties and performances. There must be a deep conviction before you can be brought out of your self-righteousness; it is the last idol taken out of our hearts. The pride of our hearts will not let us submit to the righteousness of Jesus Christ. But if you never felt that you had no righteousness of your own, if you never felt the deficiency of your own righteousness, you cannot come to Jesus Christ. There are a great many now who may say, Well, we believe all this. But there is a great difference between talking and feeling. Did you ever feel the want of a dear redeemer? Did you ever feel the want of Jesus Christ, upon the account of the deficiency of your own righteousness? And can you now say from your heart, Lord, You may justly damn me for the best duties that ever I did perform? If you are not thus brought out of self, you may speak peace to yourselves, but there is no peace.

But then, before you can speak peace to your souls, there is one particular sin you must be greatly troubled for, and yet I fear there are few of you who think what it is. It is the reigning, the damning sin of the Christian world, and yet the Christian world seldom or never thinks of it. And pray what is that? It is what most of you think you are not guilty of—and that is the sin of unbelief. Before you can speak peace to your heart, you must be troubled for the unbelief of your heart.

But, can it be supposed that any of you are unbelievers here in this churchyard, that are born in Scotland, in a reformed country, that go to church every Sabbath? Can any of you that receive the sacrament once a year—O that it were administered more often!—can it be supposed that you who had tokens for the sacrament, that you who keep up family prayer, that any of you do not believe in the Lord Jesus Christ? I appeal to your own hearts, if you would not think me uncharitable if I doubted whether any of you believed in Christ. Yet, I fear upon examination, we should find that most of you have not so much faith in the Lord Jesus Christ as the Devil himself. I am persuaded the Devil believes more of the Bible than most of us do. He believes the divinity of Jesus Christ; that is more than many who call themselves Christians do. No, he believes and trembles, and that is more than thousands among us do.

My friends, we mistake a historical faith for a true faith, wrought in the heart by the Spirit of God. You fancy you believe because you believe there is such a book as we call the Bible—because you go to church; all this you may do and have no true faith in Christ. Merely to believe there was such a person as Christ, merely to believe there is a book called the Bible will do you no good, more than to believe there was such a man as Caesar or Alexander the Great. The Bible is a sacred depository. What thanks have we to give to God for these lively oracles! But we may have these and not believe in the Lord Jesus Christ. My dear friends, there must be a principle wrought in the heart by the Spirit of the living God.

If I ask you how long it is since you believed in Jesus Christ, I suppose most of you would tell me you believed in Jesus Christ as long as ever you remember—you never did misbelieve. Then, you could not give me a better proof that you never yet believed in Jesus Christ unless you were sanctified early, as from the womb. For they that otherwise believe in Christ know there was a time when they did not believe in Jesus Christ. You say you love God with all your heart, soul, and strength. If I were to ask you how long it is since you loved God, you would say, As long as you can remember. You never hated God, you know no time when there was enmity in your heart against God. Then, unless you were sanctified very early, you never loved God in your life.

My dear friends, I am more particular in this because

it is a most deceitful delusion, whereby so many people are carried away, that they believe already. Therefore it is remarked of Mr. Marshall, giving account of his experiences, that he had been working for life. He had ranged all his sins under the Ten Commandments and then, coming to a minister, asked him the reason why he could not get peace. The minister looked at his catalog. Away, says he, I do not find one word of the sin of unbelief in all your catalog. It is the peculiar work of the Spirit of God to convince us of our unbelief—that we have no faith. Says Jesus Christ, "I will send the Comforter, and "when he is come, he will reprove the world" of the sin of unbelief; "of sin," says Christ, "because they believe not on me."

Now, my dear friends, did God ever show you that you had no faith? Were you ever made to bewail a hard heart of unbelief? Was it ever the language of your heart, Lord, give me faith. Lord, enable me to lay hold on Thee. Lord, enable me to call You my Lord and my God? Did Jesus Christ ever convince you in this manner? Did He ever convince you of your inability to close with Christ and make you to cry out to God to give you faith? If not, do not speak of peace to your heart. May the Lord awaken you and give you true, solid peace before you go hence and be no more!

Once more then: before you can speak peace to your heart, you must not only be convinced of your actual and original sin, the sins of your own righteousness, the sin of unbelief, but you must be enabled to lay hold upon the perfect righteousness, the all-sufficient righteousness, of the Lord Jesus Christ. You must lay hold by faith on the righteousness of Jesus Christ, and then you shall have peace. "Come," says Jesus, "unto me, all ye that labour and are heavy laden, and I will give you rest." This speaks encouragement to all that are weary and heavy laden. But the promise of rest is made to them only upon their coming and believing and taking Him to be their God and their all. Before we can ever have peace with God, we must be justified by faith through our Lord Jesus Christ. We must be enabled to apply Christ to our hearts. We must have Christ brought home to our souls, so that His righteousness may be made our righteousness, so that His merits may be imputed to our souls.

My dear friends, were you ever married to Jesus Christ? Did Jesus Christ ever give Himself to you? Did you ever close with Christ by a lively faith, so as to feel Christ in your hearts, so as to hear Him speaking peace to your souls? Did peace ever flow in upon your hearts like a river? Did you ever feel that peace that Christ spoke to His disciples? I pray God He may come and speak peace to you. These things you must experience.

I am now talking of the invisible realities of another world, of inward religion, of the work of God upon a poor sinner's heart. I am now talking of a matter of great importance, my dear hearers. You are all concerned in it, your souls are concerned in it, your eternal salvation is concerned in it. You may be all at peace, but perhaps the Devil has lulled you asleep into a carnal lethargy and security and will endeavor to keep you there until he gets you to hell, and there you will be awakened. But it will be dreadful to be awakened and find yourselves so fearfully mistaken when the great gulf is fixed, when you will be calling to all eternity for a drop of water to cool your tongue and shall not obtain it.

Give me leave, then, to address myself to several sorts of persons and O may God, of His infinite mercy, bless the application! There are some of you perhaps who can say, Through grace we can go along with you. Blessed be God, we have been convinced of our actual sins. We have been convinced of original sin. We have been convinced of self-righteousness. We have felt the bitterness of unbelief, and through grace we have closed with Jesus Christ. We can speak peace to our hearts because God has spoken peace to us. Can you say so? Then I will salute you, as the angels did the women the first day of the week, All hail! Fear not ye, my dear brethren, you are happy souls. You may lie down and be at peace indeed, for God has given you peace. You may be content under all the dispensations of providence, for nothing can happen to you now but what shall be the effect of God's love to your souls. You need not fear what fightings may be without, seeing there is peace within. Have you closed with Christ? Is God your friend? Is Christ your friend? Then look up with comfort; all is yours, and you are Christ's, and Christ is God's. Everything shall work together for your good. The very hairs of your heads are numbered. He that touches you touches the apple of God's eye.

But then, my dear friends, beware of resting on your first conversion. You that are young believers in Christ, you should be looking out for fresh discoveries of the Lord Jesus Christ every moment; you must not build upon your past experiences. You must not build upon a work within you, but always come out of yourselves to the righteousness of Jesus Christ outside you. You must be always coming as poor sinners to draw water out of the wells of salvation. You must be forgetting the things that are behind and be continually pressing forward to the things that are before. My dear friends, you must keep up a tender, close walk with the Lord Jesus Christ.

There are many of us who lose our peace by our untender walk. Something or other gets in between Christ and us, and we fall into darkness. Something or other steals our hearts from God, and this grieves the Holy Spirit, and the Holy Spirit leaves us to ourselves. Let me, therefore, exhort you that have peace with God to take care that you do not lose this peace. It is true, if you are once in Christ, you cannot finally fall from God: "There is therefore now no condemnation to them which are in Christ Jesus"; but if you cannot fall finally, you may fall foully and may go with broken bones all your days. Take care of backslidings; for Jesus Christ's sake, do not grieve the Holy Spirit. You may never recover your comfort while you live. O take care of going a gadding and wandering from God after you have closed with Jesus Christ.

My dear friends, I have paid dear for backsliding. Our hearts are so cursedly wicked that if you take not care, if you do not keep up a constant watch, your wicked hearts will deceive you and draw you aside. It will be sad to be under the scourge of a correcting Father; witness the visitations of Job, David, and other saints in Scripture. Let me, therefore, exhort you that have peace to keep a close walk with Christ.

I am grieved with the loose walk of those that are Christians, that have had discoveries of Jesus Christ. There is so little difference between them and other people that I scarce know which are the true Christians. Christians are afraid to speak for God—they run down with the stream. If they come into worldly company, they will talk of the world as if they were in their element. This you would not do when you had the first discoveries of Christ's love. You could talk then of Christ's love forever, when the candle of the Lord shined upon your soul. That time has been when you had something to say for your dear Lord but now you can go into company and hear others speaking about the world bold enough, and you are afraid of being laughed at if you speak for Jesus Christ. A great many people have grown conformists now in the worst sense of the word. They will cry out against the ceremonies of the church, as they may justly do. But then you are mighty fond of ceremonies in your behavior; you will conform to the world, which is a great deal worse. Many will stay until the Devil brings up new fashions. Take care, then, not to be conformed to the world.

What have Christians to do with the world? Christians should be singularly good, bold for their Lord, that all who are with you may take notice that you have been with Jesus. I would exhort you to come to a settlement in Jesus Christ, so as to have a continual abiding of God in your heart. We go building on our faith of adherence and lose our comfort but we should be growing up to a faith of assurance to know that we are God's and so walk in the comfort of the Holy Spirit and be edified.

Jesus Christ is now much wounded in the house of His friends. Excuse me in being particular; for, my friends, it grieves me more that Jesus Christ should be wounded by His friends than by His enemies. We cannot expect anything else from Deists, but for such as have felt His power to fall away, for them not to walk agreeably to the vocation wherewith they are called—by these means we bring our Lord's religion into contempt, to be a byword among the heathen. For Christ's sake, if you know Christ keep close by Him. If God has spoken peace, O keep that peace by looking up to Jesus Christ every moment. Such as have peace with God, if you are under trials, fear not, all things shall work for your good. If you are under temptations, fear not, if He has spoken peace to your hearts, all these things shall be for your good.

But what shall I say to you that have no peace with God? And these are, perhaps, the most of this congregation—it makes me weep to think of it. Most of you, if you examine your hearts, must confess that God never yet spoke peace to you. You are children of the Devil, if Christ is not in you, if God has not spoken peace to your hearts. Poor souls! What a cursed condition are you in! I would not be in your case for ten thousand thousand worlds. Why? You are just hanging over hell. What peace can you have when God is your enemy, when the wrath of God is abiding upon your poor souls? Awake, then, you that are sleeping in a false peace. Awake, you carnal professors, you hypocrites that go to church, receive the sacrament, read your Bibles, and have never felt the power of God upon your hearts. You that are formal professors, you that are baptized heathens—awake, awake, and do not rest on a false bottom.

Blame me not for addressing myself to you; indeed, it is out of love to your souls. I see you are lingering in your Sodom and wanting to stay there, but I come to you as the angel did to Lot, to take you by the hand. Come away, my dear friends—fly, fly, fly for your lives to Jesus Christ, fly to a bleeding God, fly to a throne of grace. Beg of God to break your hearts, beg of God to convince you of your actual sins, beg of God to convince you of your original sin, beg of God to convince you of your self-righteousness—beg of God to give you faith and to enable you to close with Jesus Christ.

O you that are secure, I must be a son of thunder to you, and O that God may awaken you, though it be with thunder. It is out of love, indeed, that I speak to you. I know by sad experience what it is to be lulled asleep with a false peace. Long was I lulled asleep, long did I think myself a Christian, when I knew nothing of the Lord Jesus Christ. I went perhaps farther than many of you do. I used to fast twice a week, I used to pray sometimes nine times a day, I used to receive the sacrament constantly every Lord's day. Yet I knew nothing of Jesus Christ in my heart, I knew not that I must be a new creature—I knew nothing of inward religion in my soul. And perhaps many of you may be deceived as I, poor creature, was. Therefore, it is out of love to you indeed that I speak to you.

O if you do not take care, a form of religion will destroy your souls. You will rest in it, and will not come to Jesus Christ at all. Whereas these things are only the means and not the end of religion, Christ is the end of the law for righteousness to all that believe. O, then, awake, you that are settled on your lees; awake you church professors; awake you that have a name to live, that are rich and think you want nothing, not considering that you are poor and blind and naked. I counsel you to come and buy of Jesus Christ gold, white raiment, and eyesalve.

But I hope there are some that are a little wounded. I hope God does not intend to let me preach in vain. I hope God will reach some of your precious souls and awaken some of you out of your carnal security. I hope there are some who are willing to come to Christ and are beginning to think that they have been building upon a false foundation. Perhaps the Devil may strike in and bid you despair of mercy. But fear not, what I have been speaking to you is only out of love to you—is only to awaken you and let you see your danger. If any of you are willing to be reconciled to God, God the

Father, Son, and Holy Spirit is willing to be reconciled to you.

O then, though you have no peace as yet, come away to Jesus Christ. He is our peace, He is our peacemaker—He has made peace between God and offending man. Would you have peace with God? Away, then, to God through Jesus Christ, who has purchased peace; the Lord Jesus has shed His heart's blood for this. He died for this; He rose again for this; He ascended into the highest heaven and is now interceding at the right hand of God. Perhaps you think there will be no peace for you. Why so? Because you are sinners? Because you have crucified Christ—you have put Him to open shame—you have trampled under foot the blood of the Son of God? What of all this? Yet there is peace for you.

What did Jesus Christ say of His disciples when He came to them the first day of the week? The first word He said was, "Peace be unto you." He showed them His hands and His side, and said, "Peace be unto you." It is as much as if He had said, Fear not, My disciples; see My hands and My feet how they have been pierced for your sake; therefore fear not. How did Christ speak to His disciples? "Go to my brethren," and tell brokenhearted Peter in particular, that Christ is risen, that He ascends to His Father and your Father, to His God and your God. And after Christ rose from the dead, He came preaching peace with an olive branch of peace, like Noah's dove: "Peace I leave with you." Who were they? They were enemies of Christ as well as we, they were deniers of Christ once as well as we. Perhaps some of you have backslidden and lost your peace, and you think you deserve no peace, and no more you do. But, then, God will heal your backslidings, He will love you freely.

As for you that are wounded, if you are made willing to come to Christ, come away. Perhaps some of you want to dress yourselves in your duties that are but rotten rags. No, you had better come naked as you are, for you must throw aside your rags and come in your blood. Some of you may say, I would come, but I have got a hard heart. But you will never get it made soft until you come to Christ; He will take away the heart of stone and give you a heart of flesh. He will speak peace to your souls; though you have betrayed Him, yet He will be your peace.

Shall I prevail upon any of you this morning to come to Jesus Christ? There is a great multitude of souls here; how shortly must you all die and go to judgment! Even before night, or tomorrow's night, some of you may be laid out for this kirkyard. And how will you do if you be not at peace with God—if the Lord Jesus Christ has not spoken peace to your hearts? If God speak not peace to you here, you will be damned forever. I must not flatter you, my dear friends; I will deal sincerely with your souls. Some of you may think I carry things too far. But, indeed, when you come to judgment, you will find what I say is true, either to your eternal damnation or comfort. May God influence your hearts to come to Him! I am not willing to go away without persuading you. I cannot be persuaded but God may make use of me as a means of persuading some of you to come to the Lord Jesus Christ.

O did you but feel the peace that they have that love the Lord Jesus Christ! "Great peace have they," says the psalmist, that "love thy law; and nothing shall offend them." But there is no peace to the wicked. I know what it is to live a life of sin. I was obliged to sin in order to stifle conviction. And I am sure this is the way many of you take—if you get into company, you drive off conviction. But you had better go to the bottom at once; it must be done—your wound must be searched or you must be damned.

If it were a matter of indifference, I would not speak one word about it. But you will be damned without Christ. He is the way, He is the truth and the life. I cannot think you should go to hell without Christ. How can you dwell with everlasting burnings? How can you abide the thought of living with the Devil forever? Is it not better to have some soul-trouble here than to be sent to hell by Jesus Christ hereafter? What is hell, but to be absent from Christ? If there were no other hell, that would be hell enough. It will be hell to be tormented with the Devil forever.

Get acquaintance with God, then, and be at peace. I beseech you, as a poor, worthless ambassador of Jesus Christ, that you would be reconciled to God. My business this morning, the first day of the week, is to tell you that Christ is willing to be reconciled to you. Will any of you be reconciled to Jesus Christ? Then, He will forgive you all your sins, He will blot out all your transgressions. But if you will go on and rebel against Christ, and stab Him daily—if you will go on and abuse Jesus Christ—the wrath of God you must expect will fall upon you. God will not be mocked. That which a man sows, that shall he also reap. And if you will not be at peace with God, God will not be at peace with you.

Who can stand before God when He is angry? It is a dreadful thing to fall into the hands of an angry God. When the people came to apprehend Christ, they fell to the ground when Jesus said, "I am he." And if they could not bear the sight of Christ when clothed with the rags of mortality, how will they bear the sight of Him when He is on His Father's throne? I think I see the poor wretches dragged out of their graves by the Devil. I think I see them trembling, crying out to the hills and rocks to cover them. But the Devil will say, Come, I will take you away; then they shall stand trembling before the judgment seat of Christ. They shall appear before Him to see Him once and hear Him pronounce that irrevocable sentence, "Depart from me, ye cursed." I think I hear the poor creatures saying, Lord, if we must be damned, let some angel pronounce the sentence. No, the God of love, Jesus Christ, will pronounce it.

Will you not believe this? Do not think I am talking at random, but agreeably to the Scriptures of truth. If you do not, then show yourselves men, and this morning go away with full resolution, in the strength of God, to cleave to Christ. And may you have no rest in your souls until you rest in Jesus Christ! I could still go on, for it is sweet to talk of Christ. Do you not long for the time when you shall have new bodies—when they shall be immortal and made like Christ's glorious body? And then they will talk of Jesus Christ forevermore.

But it is time, perhaps, for you to go and prepare for your respective worship, and I would not hinder any of you. My design is to bring poor sinners to Jesus Christ. O that God may bring some of you to Himself! May the Lord Jesus now dismiss you with His blessing, and may the dear Redeemer convince you that are unawakened and turn the wicked from the evil of their way! And may the love of God that passes all understanding fill your hearts. Grant this, O Father, for Christ's sake, to whom, with You and the blessed Spirit, be all honor and glory, now and forevermore. Amen.

The Work of Grace

John Daniel Jones (1865–1942) served for forty years at the Richmond Hill Congregational Church in Bournemouth, England, where he ministered the Word with a remarkable consistency of quality and effectiveness, as his many volumes of published sermons attest. A leader in his denomination, he gave himself to church extension (he helped to start thirty new churches), assistance to needier congregations, and increased salaries for the clergy. He spoke at D. L. Moody's Northfield Conference in 1919.

This sermon is from his book, *The Hope of the Gospel*, published in 1911 by Hodder and Stoughton.

John Daniel Jones

7

THE WORK OF GRACE

By the grace of God I am what I am (1 Corinthians 15:10).

IN ONE SENSE that is true of every man—believer and unbeliever, Christian and non-Christian. Whatever a man is, he is it by the grace and favor of God. We sometimes draw a distinction between the kingdom of *nature* and the kingdom of *grace*. The distinction is one that we find convenient and practically useful, but it may very easily become a false distinction if we understand by it that grace is the realm of God's working, while nature is a realm from which God's operations are excluded. As a matter of fact, God is in nature as well as grace. He is in the common events of the common day just as certainly as He is in the great spiritual experiences of life. He is all in all. He girds men, though they do not know Him. He orders their paths and their lying down. They are what they are by the divine permission and grace. Here is an illustration of what I mean right to my hand. I take up a coin of the realm and I find graven on it the words, "George V, by the grace of God King of the Britains." King, how? by succession, by hereditary right? Yes, no doubt. But in the deepest sense of all, King by the grace of God. George V is monarch of these realms only by permission and favor of God, and he will continue our monarch just so long as God permits him. By the grace of God he is what he is.

And what is true of the king is true of everyone. In God's hand our breath is, and His are all our ways. In Him we live and move and have our being, and apart from Him we should not be at all. Have you noticed that sometimes when an artist is billed to appear at some concert or other entertainment, the information is added that he appears by permission of So-and-so"? What it means, I suppose, is something like this. Sometimes impresarios bargain with artists for their entire and exclusive services. If any such artist appears under any other auspices during the term covered by his engagement, he does so by permission of the man who has bargained for the right to his exclusive services. Now that illustrates in some measure the relation between man and God. We are His people and the sheep of His pasture. He and He alone keeps our souls in life. Should God take away our breath, we die and return to our dust. Whatever we are, we are by permission of God. So it is not only true that George V is king by the grace of God, but it is equally true that you are a doctor by the grace of God, and you are a lawyer by the grace of God, and you are a merchant by the grace of God, and you are a businessman by the grace of God, and you are a mechanic by the grace of God. Believer and unbeliever, Christian and non-Christian, good and bad, they are on absolutely the same level here. Inasmuch as they would not exist at all without God, and inasmuch as their continuance from day to day depends upon God, it is true of every man that by the grace of God he is what he is.

But the word "grace" has a special meaning in my text. It means here—as indeed it means throughout the New Testament—not simply the goodwill of permission, of which I have just been speaking and which God shows to all men, even to the unthankful and evil; it means here the active and positive favor and goodwill that God shows to all those who are in Christ Jesus. The essential meaning of grace is love. But it is love with a certain connotation, love that takes a certain direction, so that it is true to say that while all grace is love, all love is not grace. I mean this: love can be shown by an equal for an equal, by a higher for a lower, by a lower for a higher; but grace can only be shown by a higher for a lower. We can love God, but it would be a blasphemous impertinence to talk about our being gracious to Him. But God is gracious to us. Grace, then, is, as Dr. Whyte says, love that flows down; it is love that stoops; it is the love of the Highest for the lowest. And so it stands in Scripture for the love of God for man. And it was that love that made Paul. "By the grace of God I am what I am."

The Energy of Grace

Now will you notice, to begin with, how Paul's words in my text imply that grace is active, operative, energizing. Grace had made Paul. We need to have enlarged ideas of the power that resides in those forces that are immaterial and spiritual. As a result of the prevailing materialism, we are inclined, as Dr. Jowett says, to think far too meanly of spiritual ministries, and to think far too highly of the more palpable ministries of the physical universe. As a matter of fact, the mere mechanical forces are insignificant from the standpoint of power and influence compared with the intellectual and spiritual. Take the one illustration of thought. What do you say of thought? Do you reduce it to a mere movement of the physical substance of the brain? Do you say it is like the flitting of a shadow—here and then gone, leaving no trace of itself behind? Why, a thought is a living creature, as Luther would say, having eyes and teeth. Let it out, it will pass from mind to mind and life to life, molding, shaping, guiding them, and you can set no bounds to its influence.

But the greatest energy of all is *grace*—God's loving thought for men. That is a truth about grace we need more clearly to realize. Grace is not a mere sentiment, it is not an amiability—it is a force, a power, an energy. "Grace, 'tis a charming sound," says one of our hymns. Yes, there is something beautiful and winsome about the very word *grace*. But I never think of that line without feeling its absurd inadequacy! Grace—a "charming sound"! Why, it would be just as appropriate to say that Niagara was a charming sound! What is the dominant impression Niagara makes as it hurries along seething, swirling, roaring to its final leap over the rocks? that of power—resistless, boundless, incalculable power! There is power in Niagara to do the work of a continent well-nigh! Ask the people of Buffalo, that great town twenty miles or so away, what Niagara is to them. And they will answer you—power! It is Niagara that runs their cars; it is Niagara that drives their machinery; it is Niagara that lights their streets. Niagara chained, harnessed, put to use, is doing the work of Buffalo. And *grace* is a perfect Niagara of power! Charming sound, indeed! It is a resistless tide of energy, it is a sweeping flood of force! That is the representation of grace given to us in the New Testament. It is not a mere sentiment, a charming sound, but an active, energizing force.

Take a reference or two in illustration of my point. "Be strengthened," writes Paul to Timothy, "in the grace that is in Christ Jesus" (RV). "Strengthened in the grace"—grace is the fountain of power and might, the secret of triumph over cowardice and fear. "God our Father . . . loved us and gave us eternal comfort and good hope through grace" (RV), writes Paul to the Thessalonians. "Eternal comfort and good hope through grace"—grace begets courage and confidence. It is like the coming of reinforcements to a sore-pressed army. It fires the heart and nerves the arm. It changes doubt and despair into the assurance of victory. We have comfort and good hope through grace. "Be not carried away by divers and strange teachings: for it is good that the heart be stablished by grace" (RV), writes the author of the epistle to the Hebrews. "Be not carried away," he says. These Hebrew Christians were being driven backward and forward by changing tides of opinion. They were like the surge of the sea—there was neither steadiness nor stability about their lives. And how was this instability of theirs to be counteracted and remedied? by grace. It was grace that would establish the heart and enable them to stand foursquare to all the winds that blew—stablished by grace.

And yet one other illustration let me give you. It is the most sweeping of them all: "God is able to make all grace abound unto you," writes Paul to the Corinthians, "that ye, having always all sufficiency in everything, may abound unto every good work" (RV). Notice the sequence! "God is able to make all grace abound unto you." Abundant grace! What next? "That ye, having always all sufficiency in everything, may abound unto every good work." Abounding grace—abounding work! Abounding grace—abounding power! Power for anything and everything! Abounding grace—always all sufficiency for everything. The apostle strains language to describe the force resident in grace—always, all sufficiency for everything! There are no impossibilities to a man reinforced and strengthened by the power of grace. "God is able to make all grace abound unto you that . . . ye may abound unto every good work."

Now this potent energy of grace had been at work in the life of Saint Paul. Ever since that memorable day when he met with Christ outside Damascus, the love of God had been the dynamic of Paul's life. "The love of Christ constraineth [me]." That love had saved him, cleansed him, comforted him, strengthened him; that love had enabled him to bear and to do and to suffer; that love had given him his knowledge, his peace, his joy. Indeed, looking back upon his life, Paul realizes that all that he has known and all that he has done, all that he is in character and power, is due entirely to the fructifying and energizing love of God. Without grace he would have been nothing; to grace he owes everything. By the grace of God I am what I am.

I want now to examine a little more closely and in detail the work of grace as illustrated in the life of Paul. "By the grace of God I am what I am," says the great apostle. What, then, had grace done for Paul?

Saved—by Grace

I answer first, grace saved him. Paul rejoices, in his epistles, that he is a sinner saved. And saved how? by grace! In speaking first of Paul's salvation, I am speaking of the very greatest thing grace did for him. If Paul had been asked, as Sir James Simpson the great Edinburgh physician was asked, what was the greatest and most welcome discovery of his whole life, he would have answered, as that great doctor answered, "The discovery that I have a Savior." Yes, the best and brightest and happiest day in all Paul's life was the day when, through Jesus Christ, he was delivered from his load of shame and sin—when he was saved by grace. If you have made any study at all of the literature of the saints, you will have noticed this: it is marked by a keen and vivid and overwhelming sense of sin. It is the very holiest of men who so realize the sinfulness of sin that they abhor themselves. Take these as illustrations:

"When I look at my sinfulness," said Samuel Rutherford, "my salvation is to me my Savior's greatest miracle. He has done nothing in heaven or on earth like my salvation."

"When a man like me," says Luther, "comes to know the plague of his own heart, he is not miserable only—he is misery itself—he is not sinful only, he is absolute sin itself."

"I am made of sin," says Bishop Andrews, in his tear-stained *Book of Prayers*.

John Bunyan has described his condition in the very title page of his book, *Grace Abounding to the Chief of Sinners, a Brief Relation of the Exceeding Mercy of God in Christ to His Poor Servant, John Bunyan*.

But none ever felt the shame and ache and torture of sin like Paul did. He was the bond slave of sin. Sin reigned over him and dwelt in him. His sin gave him continual sorrow of heart. He was a persecutor, blasphemous and injurious, and he would dispute with John Bunyan his claim to being the chief of sinners. And this sin of his made Paul's life a burden to him. His day was filled with pain, and by night he made his couch wet with tears, and day and night he cried, My sins, my sins, who shall take away my sins? And from this haunting, torturing, crushing burden of sin, grace delivered him. It was nothing he had done or could do that brought him deliverance. From first to last it was the Lord's doing. Grace had done it all. "The Son of God . . . loved me, and gave himself for me"!

"It was Paul's accustomed manner," says the immortal dreamer in his touching introduction to *Grace Abounding,* "ever to open before his judges the manner of his conversion; he would think of that day and that hour in which he first did meet with grace; for it supported him." Yes, Paul was constantly going back to the day and the hour when Christ met with him and took his sins away. And why was he always reverting to that day and that hour? Not simply, as John Bunyan says, because it supported him, and not simply in order to give glory to God. But chiefly for this reason: in order to bring hope to the sin-burdened men and women to whom he spoke. The story of Damascus was in itself the mightiest argument. Paul himself was the evidence and proof of the Gospel. There was none beyond the reach of that saving and redeeming grace which on that day and that hour saved Paul, the chief of sinners. "Where sin abounded," was the Gospel Paul preached to a groaning world, "grace did much more abound." There is no one so sunk in sin, so enslaved by sin, so defiled by sin as to be beyond the uplifting, emancipating and cleansing power of grace. "In whom we have redemption," writes the great evangelical apostle to his Ephesian converts, "through his blood, the forgiveness of sins, according to the riches of his grace." It matters not how deep our sinfulness may be—though, like Bishop Andrewes, we feel ourselves to be made of sin, though like Bunyan we fall at the sight of our own vileness deeply into despair, though like Paul we feel ourselves the chief of sinners—Christ's grace is so rich and full that it can bring redemption and forgiveness of sins to us. We are helpless to rid ourselves of the burden or to deliver ourselves from its pain—but God's free love is able to deliver and redeem. We are saved by grace.

> Thy grace, alone, O God,
>   To me can pardon speak,
> Thy power alone, O Son of God,
>   Can this sore bondage break.

An Apostle—by Grace

But salvation was not the only thing grace bestowed upon Paul. "By the grace of God I am what I am." Well, what was he? not only a sinner saved, but a Christian apostle. And how came he to be an apostle? by the grace of God. That indeed is the precise reference of my text. Paul never ceased to wonder at the marvel of his salvation. But next only to the marvel of his salvation was the marvel of his apostleship. Paul was "lost in wonder, love and praise" when he thought of his apostleship. For of all men he seemed the least worthy of this high honor and dignity. "For I am the least of all the apostles," he writes in the verse before my text, "that am not meet to be called an apostle, because I persecuted the church of God. But by the grace of God I am what I am." It was God's grace that had lifted him up to that height and conferred upon him that honor. Indeed in one place he calls his apostleship a "grace." "To me, who am less than the least of all saints, was this grace given, to preach unto the Gentiles the unsearchable riches of Christ" (RV). How was it that he who was less than the least of all saints became an apostle? by grace. Grace did more than save Paul; it brought him to honor and dignity.

And this again is one of the works of grace. This is one of the perpetually recurring effects of grace. This is a result of grace that is illustrated in the life of every Christian. It is perfectly true we do not become apostles. But it is still true, is it not, that grace does not stop its work at forgiveness but goes on to promote a man to honor and renown? Grace finds the sinner in the gutter and makes a saint of him. Paul in one of his letters speaks of men being adopted as sons through Jesus Christ unto God. What an honor is this—that men should become sons of God, and should have a mansion in the Father's house! How came such an honor to the lot of sinful men? through *grace*. We have received the adoption that we might be "to the praise of the glory of His grace." You see the grace of the father, in the parable, in forgiving the prodigal who had wasted his substance and broken his heart. But the father did not stop at mere forgiveness, did he? He went on to show the glory of his grace by giving him the best robe and a ring for his hand and shoes for his feet and restoring him to the son's place. And so you see the grace of God in the remission and forgiveness of sin, but you see the glory of His grace in this, that He sets these sin-stained men and women on thrones and gives them crowns and clothes them in white and makes them kings and priests to God. We sing sometimes about the glories of the saints, about their bliss and unspeakable joy. Once these saints in glory were like ourselves—

> They wrestled hard as we do now,
> With sins and doubts and fears;

But if we ask them,

> —whence their victory came?
> They with united breath,
> Ascribe their conquest to the Lamb,
> Their triumph to His death.

Yes, they sit on their thrones but not, shall I say, as a result of their own merit. They cry, "Not unto us, O LORD, not unto us, but unto Thy name give glory." They cast their crowns before the throne of the Lamb, and every victor confesses, "By the grace of God I am what I am."

A Successful Worker—by Grace

"By the grace of God I am what I am," says Paul. And what was Paul more than a saved sinner and a called apostle? He was also a successful worker. And how came he to be a successful worker? by the grace of God. I scarcely know where to begin when I speak of Paul as a worker. Never surely did any man toil as he did. He traveled innumerable miles, he preached innumerable sermons, he suffered unspeakable hardships. He took the whole world for his parish—and as the result of his unwearied labor he dotted all the lands between Antioch and Rome with Christian churches. He was called into the service last of all the apostles, as one indeed born out of due time. But so earnestly, so unsparingly, with such consuming zeal did he fling himself into the service, that Paul, modest man though he was, can speak in the verse of my text as having labored "more abundantly than they all." And then he at once corrects himself. He knows that his vast toil, and the success he met with were not to be put to his own credit but to the Divine love aiding him and strengthening him. "Yet not I," he adds, "but the grace of God which was with me." The excellency of the power, Paul knew, was of God and not of himself. Grace made Paul a successful worker. He knew there would never have been a church established or a soul saved but for the "grace of God that was with him."

Grace it is that makes men successful workers still. "Apart from me," said Jesus Christ, "ye can do nothing" (RV). Notice that! Apart from the Divine help we are utterly and entirely impotent. But assisted by the Divine grace there is nothing we cannot do! "If God be for us," said Paul exultingly, "who can be against us?" And again, "I can do all things through Christ which strengtheneth me." Men have attempted what looked like impossible tasks with very scanty material resources, but the grace that was bestowed upon them was not found vain. Carey went to India with a church at home indifferent to missions and a government in India opposed to his coming. He, the Northampton shoemaker, flung himself upon the ancient and hoary paganisms of that country. It seemed a mad enterprise, but the grace was not found vain. Robert Morrison did the same in China, and the grace was not found vain. Lawes and Chalmers went to the savages of New Guinea. It seemed a hopeless undertaking to Christianize New Guinea. But listen to this: "I have seen myself," said Dr. Lawes, "six murderers and cannibals live peaceful lives. I have seen shameless thieves and robbers become honest. I have seen the lascivious and filthy become pure. I have seen the quarrelsome and selfish become unselfish and kind"—the grace was not found vain. And that grace avails for us. In face of the paganism of England, in face of those multitudes of people whom the churches do not touch; in face of the work at our own doors, in the church, in the Sabbath school, in our homes, that grace will not be in vain. Let us fling ourselves upon God, and we too shall accomplish great things, and yet not we, but the grace of God that is with us.

A Steadfast Christian—by Grace

"By the grace of God I am what I am." And I had meant to have added that in addition to being a sinner saved and a called apostle and a successful worker, Paul was a persevering Christian—through grace. This same grace that redeems and calls and strengthens also keeps. Paul had his share of temptation and difficulty and trial in the Christian life. Many of those associated with him found the life too hard and turned back. But Paul never faltered. He bore up against deprivation and suffering and loss—through grace. He tells of one of his trials, a thorn in the flesh, he called it. He besought the Lord thrice to take it away. But God's reply was, "My grace is sufficient for thee." And what grace did in the case of that particular trial, it did in the case of all the trials and temptations that beset him. Grace proved sufficient, so that at the end he could say, "I have fought the good fight; I have finished the course, I have kept the faith" (RV).

And grace is still sufficient. The forces of the world all tend to drive a man into sin and shame. But here is another force that is stronger than the pressure of the world and that will keep a man pressing toward the highest and the best. A boat left to itself will naturally float with the current. If you want to drive it up the river you must have within the boat some force stronger than the force of the current, such as, for instance, the force of steam. The natural tendency for men is to go with the stream, and the stream carries us to shame and death; to breast the stream we need some force within us stronger than the world outside us, and that stronger force we have in the grace of God. We have but to receive God's grace and we, too, shall be able to keep ourselves unspotted from the world and to endure to the end. God's grace is a keeping grace. To every struggling soul, to every one who feels the fierce force of the world's temptations, God says, "My grace is sufficient for thee."

Here, then, we are surrounded by infinite redeeming, uplifting, strengthening, keeping energy. It is ours for the taking. This divine energy can be ours. When we are in Christ, all this wealth of saving force flows into us. Of His fullness we can all partake, grace instead of grace. "Now unto Him that is able to guard you from stumbling, and to set you before the presence of His glory without blemish in exceeding joy, to the only God our Saviour through Jesus Christ our Lord, be glory, majesty, dominion and power, before all time, and now, and for evermore. Amen" (RV).

NOTES

The Riches of His Grace

David Martyn Lloyd-Jones (1898–1981) was born in Wales and moved to London in 1914. There he trained for a medical career and was associated with the famous Dr. Thomas Horder in Harley Street. He abandoned medicine for the Gospel ministry, and from 1927 to 1938 he served the Presbyterian church at Sanfields, Aberavon, Wales. In 1938, he became associate minister with Dr. G. Campbell Morgan at the Westminster Chapel, London; in 1943, when Morgan retired, Lloyd-Jones succeeded him. His expositions of the Scriptures attracted great crowds wherever he preached. He retired in 1968 to devote his time to writing and limited itinerant ministry. Calvinistic in doctrine, he emphasized the "plight of man and the power of God to save."

This message is reprinted from *God's Ultimate Purpose*, published in 1979 by Baker Book House.

David Martyn Lloyd-Jones

8

THE RICHES OF HIS GRACE

> In whom we have redemption through his blood, the forgiveness of sins, according to the riches of his grace (Ephesians 1:7).

WE NOW COME to deal with the last phrase in this verse: "according to the riches of his grace." There are many ways of considering and studying the Scriptures, and it must be clear by now that I am a follower and an exponent of one particular method. I regard the Scriptures and these great statements in it as being comparable to a great art gallery where there are famous paintings hanging on the walls. Certain people, when they visit such a place, buy a catalog from the guide at the door and then holding it in their hands walk around the gallery. They notice that item number one is a painting by Van Dyck, let us say; and they say "Ah, that is a Van Dyck." Then they pass on hurriedly to item number two, which is perhaps a portrait by Rembrandt. "Ah," they say, "that's a Rembrandt, a famous picture." Then they move on to further items in the same way. I grant that that is a possible way of viewing the treasures of an art gallery. Yet I have a feeling that when such people have gone through every room of the gallery and have said, "Well, we have 'done' the National Gallery, let us now go to the Tate Gallery," the truth is that they have never really seen either of the galleries or their treasures. It is the same in regard to the Scriptures. There are people who walk through this first chapter of this epistle to the Ephesians in some such manner as I have described, and they feel that they have "done" it. It is surely better to stand, if necessary, for hours before this chapter that has been given to us by God Himself through His Spirit and to gaze upon it and to try to discover its riches both in general and in detail. The Scriptures are meant to feed our souls, to enrich our minds, and to move our hearts. If we are to know such experiences we must tarry with these things, we must drink them in and take of their fullness.

Let us then stand and look at this particular statement: "according to the riches of his grace." Surely every true Christian must desire to stop here. Surely the apostle as he wrote under the inspiration of the Spirit expected the people to whom he wrote to meditate upon and to pray over and to think about this phrase until their hearts should be ravished by it, even as his undoubtedly was when he wrote it. Let us start by noting the way in which the apostle comes to this particular statement. He has first of all reminded us that the method or mode of our salvation is by the payment of a ransom. Next he tells us that the first thing we realize and appreciate as a result of our deliverance is "the forgiveness of sins." But he cannot leave it there. What is it that makes all this possible? What is it that gives us this salvation by ransom, this forgiveness of sins, that we enjoy? The answer, as it always must be, is "the riches of his grace"!

In a sense the apostle has already been saying as much. He hints at it in the very first verse; he implies it throughout. He himself is an apostle "by the will of God," which is just another way of saying "by the grace of God"; for if God had not been a God of grace He could never have willed such a thing for such a man. But as he refers to it once more we notice that there is one change. In verse 6, for instance, the apostle has used the term "grace"—"to the praise of the glory of his grace." But here he speaks of the "riches of his grace." Grace, as he thinks of it in verse 6, is one of the manifestations of the glory of God; it is one of the facets of that eternal brightness that flashes upon us. Everything in God is glorious. His glory is manifested in an infinite variety of ways; grace is one of them, and one of the most notable. So as we read of "the glory of his grace" in verse 6, here there is this change to "the riches of his grace." Why the change? For this reason: in the sixth verse, as a part of the whole statement of verses 3–6, the apostle was looking at salvation from the Godward angle or standpoint. And there, naturally, the thing that strikes him above all else is the glory of God's grace. But here he has started thinking of us and the forgiveness of our sins; he is looking at salvation from the manward aspect. Grace whenever it is looked at from the manward side, must always convey to us this idea of riches. Hence the apostle introduces "riches" at this point.

This is one of the apostle's most characteristic statements. Indeed, it is his favorite statement. In the second chapter, verse 4, he says, "But God, who is *rich* in mercy, for his great love wherewith he loved us." Then in the seventh verse of that chapter he says, "That in the ages to come he might show the exceeding *riches* of his grace in his kindness toward us through Christ Jesus." Again, in the third chapter, in the eighth verse he says, "Unto me, who am less than the least of all saints, is this grace given, that I should preach among the Gentiles the unsearchable *riches* of Christ." This theme obviously filled the mind and the heart of this great apostle. It was something that ravished his heart. As Philip Doddridge assures us, grace was to him "a charming sound, harmonious to the ear." It ravished his heart and moved his entire being. He never mentions grace without going into some kind of ecstasy. The word always calls forth his superlatives. It had so gripped him and amazed him and moved him that he could scarcely control himself.

Such jubilation is not surprising in view of the wonderful thing that had happened to Paul on the road to Damascus. He never ceased to wonder that he who had been a persecutor and a blasphemer and an injurious person, insulting the person of Christ, he who had thought with himself that he ought to do many things contrary to the name of Jesus of Nazareth, he who had been a self-satisfied, proud, contented Pharisee, boasting of and smug in the contemplation of his abounding self-righteousness—that he of all men should ever have been forgiven and, moreover, called to be an apostle, made a preacher of the Gospel, and sent out as the Lord's special emissary to the Gentiles. That he, of all men, should be the subject of the grace of God was truly an amazing fact, and as he looked at himself he was ever amazed.

The apostle seems to ask himself, "Is it possible? Am I still Saul of Tarsus? Am I still the same man? And if I am, what accounts for my being what I am now?" And there was only one answer: I am what I am by the grace of God. The *riches* of his grace! His greatest desire in life was that all might know this, that everyone might experience the riches of God's grace. In the third chapter of this Epistle, verse 8, he describes his calling: "Unto me, who am less than the least of all saints, is this grace given, that I should preach among the Gentiles the unsearchable riches of Christ." The grace that made him a preacher drove him across continents and across seas; it made him preach day and night with tears and pleading; it was the most vital force in his life. This was the thing that constrained him, and made him say, "Woe is unto me, if I preach not the gospel!" He was driven by the thought of these riches of God's grace and the ignorance of men and women concerning them. It was his chief reason for writing this epistle to the Ephesians.

Paul tells the Ephesians that he is writing to them because they are constantly in his mind and that he is always praying for them—"the eyes of your understanding being enlightened; that ye may know . . . the riches of the glory." A similar statement occurs in the third chapter where he says, "For this cause I bow my knees unto the Father of our Lord Jesus Christ, of whom the whole family in heaven and earth is named, that he would grant you, according to the riches of his glory, to be strengthened with might by his Spirit in the inner man"—the apostle's purpose being that they might "know the love of Christ, which passeth knowledge" in its height and depth and length and breadth. In other words, he wants them to know the *riches* of God's grace.

I would ask a question at this point: Do we individually know the riches of God's grace? Have we any experience of them? Are we aware of them? I am not asking whether we have all read the epistle to the Ephesians; I am asking whether we know individually the riches of God's grace. Let us put ourselves to the following tests. To know the riches of God's grace invariably leads to the same result, in some measure, as it did in the case of Paul. It makes us sing, it makes us praise God, it makes us rejoice "with joy unspeakable and full of glory." It was because he knew these riches that the apostle writes about them, prays about them, goes into ecstasies about them, and produces his superlatives. "What can I say?" he seems to ask, "how can I express what it all means?"

Note Paul's verbs and adjectives. He says that God has caused grace to "abound" toward us; he talks about the riches of His grace; he talks about the "unsearchable riches of Christ." Language seems to be inadequate, the thing itself is so enthralling. And this is not confined to the apostle. The same exuberance is found in Christian hymns. John Wesley translated a hymn of Count Zinzendorf, and in it we find the expression, "boundless mercy." There is no limit, no end, to it. His brother Charles writes similarly—

'Tis mercy all, immense and free,
For, O my God, it found out me!

And Isaac Watts agrees when he writes, "When I survey the wondrous Cross." He does not merely say that he has looked at the Cross; he stands and surveys it; he stops there transfixed by it. This is the characteristic response of all the saints in all ages and irrespective of any natural differences that may be found in them.

I press the question as to whether we really know these riches of grace and glory. I am increasingly convinced that it is our failure at this point that accounts for many of our troubles and problems and failures.

Our lives as Christians are too often "bound in shallows and in miseries." How different we are from the New Testament people. Where is the note of triumph and of joy and of praise and of thanksgiving? Are our hearts moved and ravished? It is not that I am concerned about feelings or ecstasies as such, but I assert that no one can appreciate the wealth and riches of God's grace without responding to it in amazement. One of the most delicate and sensitive tests of our Christian profession is the extent to which we are amazed by the riches of God's grace—"Love so amazing, so divine." Have we appreciated these riches? It is because so many of us have not done so that we are constantly grumbling and complaining that we cannot see this or understand that. It explains also why many are miserable and look miserable, and therefore never attract a soul to Christ.

As we come to investigate these riches I can only indicate certain aspects or items, trusting that the sight of them will lead us to thought and to meditation and to contemplation that will go on increasing until we find ourselves "lost in wonder, love and praise."

How can we attempt to estimate and compute this great wealth? In a sense we are assaying an impossible task, because the apostle himself has said, "to know the love of Christ, which passeth knowledge." But the fact that we can never span it and comprehend it fully does not mean that we should not look at it at all. Let us go as far as we can at the present time and then go on from there as day follows day, until time is no more. I believe that our eternity will be spent in that way. That is heaven, it seems to me. The glory of eternity will be our discoveries of fresh aspects of these riches and the entering into further wonderful appreciations of the glory of God's grace.

The first test, I suggest, is that we discover the worth and the value of anything by knowing the price that was paid for it. This is a good test of a painting, a picture, or any work of art. What is it valued at? What is the price that has to be paid before it can be possessed? We have already considered the matter, but God forbid that we should be so mechanical in our thinking as to say that because we have considered it once, we need never mention it again. There should never be a service or a meeting of Christians without our mentioning the precious blood of Christ: "In whom we have redemption through his blood." I fail to understand Christians who stay at home on Sunday nights saying, "Ah, we need not attend tonight's service; we know all about the evangelistic message." Do you know all about the blood of Christ? Do you feel that you really know so much about it that you can learn nothing fresh about it? A Christian who does not receive something in an evangelistic service is, to put it at its very lowest, in a most unhealthy condition. If your heart is not made to beat faster every time you hear about the blood of Christ you are not like the apostle Paul. The riches of God's grace are seen in the price that was paid for our redemption—"In whom we have redemption through his blood," not gold or silver or platinum, not any of the world's most precious metals; but the blood of the Son of God, the poured-out life of Him by whom all things were made, and by whom all things consist. That is one way of estimating the riches of God's grace.

The second way of appreciating the riches is to note the munificent way in which God gives us these riches. That is, in itself, an expression of the greatness of the riches. We have "redemption through his blood, . . . according to the riches of his grace." All we have is not the result of our requests to God; it is freely given by God. If you go to a wealthy person and make a request for a gift, and he, having considered it, says, "Very well, I will give it to you," you are very grateful, and rightly so. It proves that he is a generous person. But when we come to think of this great salvation, all lesser giving pales in significance. God does not forgive us because we ask Him to forgive us. God did not send His Son into the world because mankind kept on pleading with Him to do so. Nothing in salvation is given to us by God by way of response to a request from us, nothing whatsoever! It is all and entirely and absolutely from God. He has given without being asked; He has poured it out without any request. It is, indeed, in spite of us, in spite of our being enemies and aliens and rebels, in spite of our turning our backs upon Him. It is in spite of all we are and all that we have done that God has given us the riches of his grace. The initiative as well as the giving is entirely His.

Then we must go on to realize that the apostle is emphasizing here that God gives all this to us not in a grudging manner but with a liberality and largesse that baffles description. James conveys an idea of this to us in the first chapter of his epistle when he tells us that if any of us lack wisdom we should ask God who "giveth . . . liberally and upbraideth not." If I may say so with reverence, God cannot give in any other way. God does not give grudgingly; His nature makes that impossible. God must be liberal. Because He is God, He can only act in one manner, and that is that He gives with fullness, with freedom, with superabundance, without let or hindrance or limit. As we have already seen, the apostle Paul in Ephesians 3 says that God's way of giving "passeth knowledge." He talks there about measurements, about height and depth and length and breadth. As we live in time, we instinctively think of vastness in terms of measures. We measure it with the help of telescopes, theodolites, and other instruments. So the apostle, as it were, invites us to bring all our instruments and all our agencies, and with them try to measure God's love and goodness to us. But he assures us that it is all futile. Go as far as you can and still you have not even begun; it passeth knowledge. God's love and grace are a never-ebbing sea. You may think that you see across it, and you launch out into it only to discover that there is still another horizon and then another and another and another; it is endless, it is a vast abyss, it passeth knowledge. The riches of His grace are as large and as great and as profound as God Himself, for when God prepared our salvation He gave

Himself in His Son. So the riches of God's grace is really God Himself. He has treasured up all His treasures of wisdom and of grace in the Son; all is in Christ. The measure of the riches of God's grace is the measure of the person of God. So we can say, in our puny, inadequate language, that the riches of God's grace are unfathomable. As William Cowper reminds us in one of his hymns:

> Deep in unfathomable mines
> Of never-failing skill,
> He treasures up His bright designs,
> And works His sovereign will.

Whenever we explore the words and ways and works of God we find ourselves in a large and "wealthy place," as the psalmist reminds us (66:12). The riches of God's grace are inexhaustible, and although the saints of the centuries have been drinking out of this fountain, it is as full as it was at the beginning. Millions yet will drink out of it, but it will be still bubbling up to the surface. It matters not what your need or problem may be; there is nothing that can ever afflict the human heart or the human life for which provision has not already been made. Jesus does all things well (Mark 7:37). If any man comes to Me, says Christ, he will never thirst again (John 4:4). Never, never thirst! He is the all-sufficient one, and all who come to Him are fully satisfied.

We must next look at some of the details of these riches of God's grace. First of all there is what the apostle has already mentioned—free forgiveness, forgiveness without any payment whatsoever. He demands nothing. His invitation is, "Ho, everyone that thirsteth, come ye to the waters, . . . come, buy . . . without money and without price" (Isaiah 55:1). There are some who are unhappy in their spiritual lives because they have not realized that first truth. They are still trying to bring some kind of money, some kind of payment. They say, "I am not good enough yet, I am trying to be." There is only one thing to say to such a person: salvation is without money and without price—not a farthing, not a cent! Nothing is demanded as payment and nothing will be received as payment. It is all by the riches of His grace. Is there anything more insulting to a person who is giving you a gift out of the largeness of his heart than to put your hand in your pocket and to say, "I would like to give you something for that." We have all been insulting the almighty God by trying to offer Him something. Realize that salvation is the result of the riches of His grace.

> Just as I am, without one plea
> > But that Thy blood was shed for me,
>
> And that Thou bid'st me come to Thee,
> > O Lamb of God, I come.
>
> Nothing in my hand I bring;
> > Simply to Thy cross I cling;
>
> Naked, come to Thee for dress;
> > Helpless, look to Thee for grace;
>
> Foul, I to the fountain fly,
> > Wash me, Saviour, or I die.

That is the language of the Christian.

Again, God's forgiveness is always a full forgiveness. That is still more marvelous. When God forgives us our sins He keeps nothing at all back. There is no reservation and there are no conditions. He does not say, "Now I am going to forgive you on condition"—never! "I forgive you," says God, "because my Son bore the punishment of your sins." He justifies us freely, fully; our past sins are forgiven, our present sins are forgiven, our future sins are already dealt with there. O the riches of His grace! If we belong to His Son, God's book of the law is put on one side; that ledger will never be brought out again as far as we are concerned. We are justified once and forever. It is a full forgiveness.

More than that, it is a complete reconciliation to God. If you believe on the Lord Jesus Christ, if you believe that He has died for your sins and borne your punishment, if you are resting only upon Him, I proclaim authoritatively to you that you have a complete reconciliation to God. There is nothing now between you and God because Christ has died for you. You have been fully restored to the fellowship of God and fitted to enjoy as much as Adam enjoyed before he fell. Yes, more, because you are in Christ! Are you enjoying this full fellowship with God? When you go to God in prayer do you go with a craven spirit, hesitant and doubtful, or do you go realizing that the way to God is wide open by the blood of Jesus? Such is the teaching of the Scripture, and it is an aspect of the riches of His grace.

I fear that many of us are like the prodigal son. In desperation we go back home, and we believe certain things. But how inadequate was the prodigal's idea and conception of his father's love. He went in fear and trembling saying, "Father, I . . . am no more worthy to be called thy son: make me as one of thy hired servants." "What are you talking about?" says the father, in effect. "Bring out the best robe, bring out the ring, go and kill the fatted calf." That is God's way. It is full reconciliation; it is as if the prodigal had never done any wrong, as if he had never insulted his father before he left home, as if he had never left home at all. Everything is forgotten and banished; the reconciliation is complete. That is now our relationship to God in Christ Jesus. If we are trusting in Christ we are fully reconciled.

But the riches of God's grace go even beyond that! Not only is all this true of us, we can also know it to be true. We can have knowledge of it and assurance of it and certainty concerning it here and now. It would still be a marvelous and a wonderful thing if God had reconciled us in Christ and had not told us that He had done so. It would be a wonderful thing if all of us when we come to die should have a sudden surprise and find that, although all through our lives we had felt that we had so sinned against God that He could not forgive us and in consequence had been miserable and unhappy, God had already forgiven us ever since we first believed in His Son. That would be marvelous, but God does not deal with us in such a manner. In the riches of God's grace, He not only forgives us, but also tells us that He has done so. We can have full assurance of faith and of hope, even in this world. We rejoice that being justified by faith, we have peace with God. He is a poor Christian who does not know that his sins are forgiven. We have no right to be lacking in assurance of salvation; it is our birthright. God has given it; it is a part of His purpose for us; it is an aspect of the superabundance that He gives us "according to the riches of His grace.

Then think of our sonship and the adoption to which we have already referred. Consider them again and do not say foolishly, "We have done with adoption." Go back and contemplate that truth until you find yourself on your feet praising God. Then remind yourself once more of what it means to be "in Christ." And yet again, consider the gift of the Holy Spirit and our being sealed by the Spirit of God until the time of the redemption of the purchased possession. Make sure that you know something of the power of the Holy Spirit working in you. The apostle prayed that these Ephesians might have that knowledge. He desired that they might know the "exceeding greatness of his power to us-ward who believe" (1:19). God does not save us and forgive our sins and then leave us to ourselves to fight the world, the flesh, and the Devil. He has given us the gift of the Spirit. By the Spirit, Christ dwells in us, and He is "able to do [for us] exceeding abundantly above all that we ask or think" (3:20). When you tend to feel oppressed by the Devil and the world and the flesh, remember the power that brought Christ up again from the dead and that is working in you now according to the riches of His grace.

Then go on to remind yourself of what the apostle says in the second chapter about our having access into the presence of God as the result of the riches of His grace. "For through him [Christ] we both have access by one Spirit unto the Father" (v. 18). Heaven means being in the presence of God and enjoying Him without let or hindrance or restraint and the apostle reminds us that according to the riches of God's grace we are given a foretaste of that blessing here in this world. We have access to the Father by Christ, through the Spirit. Do you know God? Are you enjoying God? Are you enjoying a life of fellowship with God? Do you know that God intends you to have that joy? You must not be content with anything less. You must believe these words, you must believe the message. Do not wait for a special feeling; take the Word of God as it is and act upon it. God Himself has made this possible for us, and we are to receive of these riches.

The apostle also writes about Christ dwelling in our hearts by faith. Indeed, he goes on to say something still more astounding. We are to "know the love of Christ, which passeth knowledge, that [we] might be filled with all the fulness of God" (3:19). With Charles Wesley, there is nothing we are able to say at this point except, "Who can explore His strange design?" But we are to know, to experience, and to enjoy it more and more. The fullness of God! Christ in our hearts by faith! Spiritual manifestations of the Son of God, times when He comes to you and you know that He is there! This does not mean that you see Him with the naked eye but that you know and feel that He is present. All this is offered us according to the riches of His grace. It is not surprising that John Cennick in his hymn should exhort us, saying

> Children of the heavenly King,
> As ye journey, sweetly sing.

Isaac Watts encourages us to do so by reminding us that "celestial fruit" can grow even on this earthly ground on which we live. This is how he expresses it:

> The men of grace have found
> Glory begun below;
> Celestial fruit on earthly ground
> From faith and hope may grow.

> The hill of Zion yields
> A thousand sacred sweets,
> Before we reach the heavenly fields,
> Or walk the golden streets.
>
> There shall we see His face
> And never, never sin;
> There from the rivers of His grace
> Drink endless pleasures in,
>
> Then let our songs abound,
> And every tear be dry:
> We're marching through Immanuel's ground
> To fairer worlds on high.

It is in this world, says the apostle, that we are to taste the firstfruits of the great harvest and have a foretaste of the great feast that God has prepared for us in all its fullness in heaven.

Again, think of the armor that the apostle speaks of in the last chapter of this epistle. Everything necessary to enable us to stand in the evil day against the wiles of Satan is provided for us; every part of us is covered completely.

Such are some of the riches of God's grace. And all this, of course, leads to joy and to peace and love. It also leads to a sense of security and of safety, and all, remember, is simply with reference to our lives in this world and in time. Then lift up your eyes and see awaiting us, "the hope of his calling" and "the riches of the glory of his inheritance in the saints," the "inheritance incorruptible and undefiled and that fadeth not away, reserved in heaven "for us who are in Christ. It is all prepared, and it is all a part of the riches of His grace. We shall see Him as He is, and we shall be with Him, we shall reign with Him, we shall enjoy Him, we shall be like Him and lords of the universe with Him. When we return to God in repentance and faith we do not do so as servants, for we are adopted sons! And we are to enjoy all that our Father's heart and love have prepared for us. That is what is offered us in Christ Jesus according to the riches of God's grace.

What is there for us to say as we contemplate all this but,

> Just as I am, and waiting not
> To rid my soul of one dark blot,
> To Thee, whose blood can cleanse each spot,
> O Lamb of God, I come.
>
> Just as I am, poor, wretched, blind;
> Sight, riches, healing of the mind,
> Yea, all I need, in Thee to find,
> O Lamb of God, I come.

Poor pauper! Rise up, and in your rags and penury go to Him and begin to receive the riches of His grace. Believe Him when He tells you that all this and infinitely more is available now. Hold out your hand and receive it, and you will soon be rejoicing and amazed at the riches of His grace.

The Riches of Grace

Alexander Maclaren (1826–1910) was one of Great Britain's most famous preachers. While pastoring the Union Chapel, Manchester (1858–1903), he became known as "the prince of expository preachers." Rarely active in denominational or civic affairs, Maclaren invested his time in studying the Word in the original languages and sharing its truths with others in sermons that are still models of effective expository preaching. He published a number of books of sermons and climaxed his ministry by publishing his monumental *Expositions of Holy Scripture*.

This message is taken from *Expositions of Holy Scripture*, reprinted in 1974 by Baker Book House, volume 13.

Alexander Maclaren

9

THE RICHES OF GRACE

> That in the ages to come he might shew the exceeding riches of his grace in kindness toward us in Christ Jesus (Ephesians 2:7 RV).

ONE VERY STRIKING characteristic of this epistle is its frequent reference to God's purposes, and what, for want of a better word, we must call His *motives* in giving us Jesus Christ. The apostle seems to rise even higher than his ordinary height while he gazes up to the inaccessible light and with calm certainty proclaims not only what God has done, but why He has done it. Through all the earlier portions of this letter the things on earth are contemplated in the light of the things in heaven. The great work of redemption is illuminated by the thought of the will and meaning of God therein. For example, we read in chapter 1 that He "hath blessed us with all spiritual blessings, in Christ: according as he hath chosen us in him." Immediately after we read that He has "predestinated us unto the adoption of children by Jesus Christ . . . according to the good pleasure of his will." Soon after, we hear that "he hath revealed to us the mystery of his will, according to his good pleasure which he hath purposed in himself," and that our predestination to an inheritance in Christ is "according to the purpose of him who worketh all things after the counsel of his own will."

Not only so, but the motive or reason for the divine action in the gift of Christ is brought out in a rich variety of expression as being "the praise of the glory of his grace" (1:6), or that "he might gather together in one all things in Christ" (1:10), or that "we should be to the praise of his glory" (1:12), or that "unto the principalities and powers in heavenly places might be known by the church the manifold wisdom of God."

In like manner our text follows a sublime statement of what has been bestowed upon men in Jesus with an equally sublime insight into the divine purpose of showing "the exceeding riches of His grace." Such heights are not for our unaided traversing. It is neither reverent nor safe to speculate and still less to dogmatize, concerning the meaning of the divine acts. But here, at all events, we have, as I believe, not a man making unwarranted assertions about God's purposes, but God Himself, by a man, letting us see so far into the depths of Deity as to know the very deepest meaning of His very greatest acts. When God speaks, it is neither reverent nor safe to refuse to listen.

The Purpose of God in Christ Is the Display of His Grace

Of course we cannot speak of motives in the divine mind as in ours. They imply a previous state of indecision and an act of choice, from which comes the slow emerging of a resolve like that of the moon from the sea. A given end being considered by us desirable, we then cast about for means to secure it, which again implies limitation of power. Still we can speak of God's motives, if only we understand, as this epistle puts it so profoundly, that His is an eternal purpose that he purposed in himself, which never began to be formed and was not formed by reason of anything external.

With that caution Paul would have us think that God's chiefest purpose in all the wondrous facts that make up the Gospel is the setting forth of Himself, and that the chiefest part of Himself, which He desires that all men should come to know, is the glory of His grace. Of course very many and various reasons for acts may be alleged, but this is the deepest of them all. It has often been misunderstood and made into a very hard and horrible doctrine, which really means little else than almighty selfishness, but it is really a most blessed one. It is the proclamation in tenderest, most heart-melting fashion of the truth that God is love and therefore delights in imparting that which is

His creatures' life and blessedness. It bids us think that He, too, amidst the blessedness of His infinite Being, knows the joy of communicating that makes so large a part of the blessedness of our finite selves and that He, too, is capable of being touched and gladdened by the joy of expression. As an artist in his noblest work paints or chisels simply for love of pouring out his soul, so, but in infinitely loftier fashion, the great Artist delights to manifest Himself and in manifesting to communicate somewhat of Himself. Creation is divine self-revelation, and we might say with all reverence that God acts as birds sing and fountains leap and stars shine.

But our text leads us still farther into mysteries of glory when it defines what it is in God that he most desires to set forth. It is the "exceeding riches his of grace," in which wonderful expression we note that apostle's passionate accumulation of epithets that he yet feels to be altogether inadequate to his theme. It would carry us too far to attempt to bring out the whole wealth contained in these words that glide so easily over unthinking lips, but we may lovingly dwell for a few moments upon them. *Grace,* in Paul's language, means love lavished upon the undeserving and sinful, a love that is not drawn forth by the perception of any excellence in its objects but wells up and out like a fountain by reason of the impulse in its subject and that in itself contains and bestows all good and blessing. There may be, as this very letter shows, other aspects of the divine nature that God is glad that man should know. His power and His wisdom have their noblest illustration in the work of Jesus and are less conspicuously manifested in all His work. But His grace is shrined in Christ alone and from Him flows forth into a thirsty world. That love, unmerited and free, holds in solution power, wisdom, and all the other physical or metaphysical perfections belonging to God, with all their energies. It is the elixir in which they are all contained, the molten splendor into which have been dissolved gold and jewels and all precious things. When we look at Christ, we see the divinest thing in God and that is His grace. The Christ who shows us and certifies to us the grace of God must surely be more than man. Men look at Him and see it; He shows us that grace because He was full of grace and truth.

Paul is here not propounding theological dogmas but pouring out a heart full of personal experience and so adds yet other words to express what he himself has found in the divine grace and speaks of its riches. He has learned fully to trust its fullness, and in his own daily life has had the witness of its inexhaustible abundance which remains the same after all its gifts. It "operates unspent." That continually self-communicating love pours out in no narrower stream to its last recipient than to its first. All eat and are filled, and after they are satisfied, twelve baskets full of fragments are taken up. These riches are exceeding; they surpass all human conception, all parallel, all human needs; they are properly transcendent.

This, then, is what God would have us know of Himself. So His love is at once the motive of His great message to us in Jesus Christ and is the whole contents of the message, like some fountain, the force of whose transparent waters cleanses the earth and rushes into the sunshine, being at once the reason for the flow and that which flows. God reveals because He loves, and His love is that which He reveals.

The Great Manifestation of Grace Is God's Kindness to Us in Christ

All the revelation of God in creation and providence carries the same message, but it is often there hard to decipher, like some half-obliterated inscription in a strange tongue. In Jesus the writing is legible, continuous, and needs no elaborate commentary to make its meaning intelligible. But we may note that what the apostle founds on here is not so much Christ in Himself as that which men receive in Christ. As he puts it in another part of this epistle, it is "through the church" (RV) that "principalities and powers in heavenly places" are made to know "the manifold wisdom of God." It is "His kindness toward us" by which to "the ages to come," is made known the exceeding riches of His grace. That kindness can be best estimated by thinking what we were, namely, dead in trespasses and sins; what we are, namely, quickened together in Christ, raised up with Him, and with Him made to sit in heavenly places, as the immediately preceding clauses express it. All this marvelous transformation of conditions and of self is realized "in Christ Jesus." These three words recur over and over again in this profound epistle, and may be taken as its very keynote. It would carry us beyond all limits to deal with the various uses and profound meanings of this phrase in this letter. But we may at least point out how intimately and inseparably it is intertwined with the other aspect of our relations to Christ in which He is mainly regarded as dying for us and may press upon you that these two are not, as they have sometimes been taken to be, antagonistic but complementary. We shall never understand the depths of the one apostolic conception unless we bring it into closest connection with the other. Christ is for us only if we are in Christ; we are in Christ only because He died for us.

God's kindness is all "in Christ Jesus" (RV). In Him is the great channel through which His love comes to men, the river of God that is full of water. And that kindness is realized by us when we are in Christ. Separated from Him we do not possess it; joined to Him as we may be by true faith in Him, it is ours, and with it all the blessings that it brings into our else empty and thirsting hearts. Now all this sets in strong light the dignity and work of Christian people; the profundity and clearness of their religious character is the great sign to the world of the love of God. The message of Christ to man lacks one chief evidence of its worth if they who profess to have received it do not, in their lives, show its value. The characters of Christian people are in every age the clearest and most effectual witnesses of the power of the Gospel. God's honor is in their hands. The starry heavens are best seen by reflecting telescopes, which, in their field, mirror the brightness above.

The Manifestation of God Through Men "in Christ" Is for All Ages

In our text the ages to come open up into a vista of undefined duration. Just as in another place in this epistle Paul regards the church as witnessing to the principalities and powers in heavenly places, so here he regards it as the perennial evidence to all generations of the ever-flowing riches of God's grace. Whatever may have been the apostle's earlier expectations of the speedy coming of the Day of the Lord, here he obviously expects the world to last through a long stretch of undefined time and for all its changing epochs to have an unchanging light. That standing witness, borne by men in Christ of the grace that has been so kind to them, is not to be antiquated nor superseded but is as valid today as when these words gushed from the heart of Paul. Eyes that cannot look upon the sun can see it as a golden glory, tingeing the clouds that lie cradled around it. And as long as the world lasts, so long will Christian people be God's witnesses to it.

There are then two questions of infinite importance to us. Do we show in character and conduct the grace that we have received by reverently submitting ourselves to its transforming energy? We need to be very close to Him for ourselves if we would worthily witness to others of what we have found Him to be. We have but too sadly marred our witness and have been like dim reflectors around a lamp that have received but little light from it and have communicated even less than we have received. Do we see the grace that shines so brightly in Jesus Christ? God longs that we should so see; He calls us by all endearments and by loving threats to look to that incarnation of Himself. And when we lift our eyes to behold, what is it that meets our gaze? Intolerable light? The blaze of the white throne? Power that crushes our puny might? No! The "exceeding riches of his grace." The voice cries, "Behold your God!" and what we see is, "In the midst of the throne . . . a Lamb as it had been slain."

How to Be Saved

William E. Sangster (1900–1960) was the "John Wesley of his generation" as he devoted his life to evangelism and the promotion of practical sanctification. He pastored in England and Wales, and his preaching ability attracted the attention of the Methodist leaders. He ministered during World War II at Westminster Central Hall, London, where he pastored the church, managed an air-raid shelter in the basement, and studied for his Ph.D. at the London University. He served as president of the Methodist Conference (1950) and director of the denomination's home missions and evangelism ministry. He published several books on preaching, sanctification, and evangelism, as well as volumes of sermons.

This message comes from *Evangelical Sermons of Our Day*, compiled by Andrew W. Blackwood and published by Harper and Brothers, New York, 1959.

William E. Sangster

10
HOW TO BE SAVED

By grace are ye saved through faith (Ephesians 2:8).

THIS WAS ONE of the great texts of the Evangelical Revival. It was Martin Luther's mighty watchword. If Spurgeon was suddenly called upon to preach, he found himself most forceful with this theme. Among John Wesley's famous forty-four sermons, the first is an exposition of this sentence from Paul.

Let me take the text in hand my own way, as every man must give his own message. This evening I propose to examine this grand verse by scrutinizing in turn each of the three key words. If we can understand what Paul meant by each of these words and what the evangelical preachers of all ages have meant, we shall find that, however the text has been neglected in recent years, this is still the marrow of the Gospel for those of us who believe.

The Word *Grace*

"By grace are ye saved." What do we mean by *grace?* The old definition called it "the free, unmerited favor of God." On that definition I cannot improve. It means that at the heart of all true communion with God there lies this deep truth, that God Himself took the initiative. He loves us better than we can ever love Him. He loves us with a love that does not depend on any answering love of ours. We have not to earn His love any more than we earned our mothers' love. We have but to receive it.

Always the initiative is from God! When you first came to Him, if indeed you have come to Him, you came because He first drew you. The very faith by which you lay hold of Him is not of yourself, this also is a gift of God. Nor is it only in the beginning that your salvation is God's free gift. Every onward step you have made in your spiritual pilgrimage has been possible by some bestowing of His grace. Even the life of holiness, to which all the time He is seeking to bring you—the Christlike quality that He wants to repeat in all of His children—even that you have not to achieve but to receive. It is a gift of God.

I know very well that such teaching affronts the modern man and that many people reject it. The man in the street rejects it tacitly. He may have had nothing to do with religion, but whenever death is mentioned he thinks to himself: "Well, I've never done anyone a bad turn!" In his own mind he believes that, not having been a flagrant sinner, he can work his passage to heaven by the good turns that he has done. I know how our church fathers would have commented on that!

I don't know that any of them ever used this illustration, but I feel sure that something of the sort would have crossed their minds. They would have imagined a man in debt for perhaps half a million pounds but refusing the help of any friend and seeking to meet his liabilities by hoarding up his farthings and coming at last to the audit with elevenpence-halfpenny to set over against a debt of half a million pounds!

There is in man something that rejects the idea of this free and generous forgiving. Of course it is pride, the deadliest of all the deadly sins. Bernard Shaw may in some things, I suppose, be taken as an example of the modern mind. He says, "Forgiveness is a beggar's refuge. We must pay our debts." So speaks the modern man, but, my dear friends, we cannot pay our debts. We shall never be able to pay our debts to God. As our spiritual fathers saw so clearly, the only language that we can honestly use in the presence of our awful debt is this prayer:

> Just as I am, without one plea
> But that Thy blood was shed for me,
> And that Thou bidd'st me come to Thee,
> O Lamb of God, I come.

In response to this coming, the free, unmerited favor of God comes to us, cancels the debt, imputes the righteousness of Christ to sinners such as we are, and progressively, as we live with Him, also imparts that righteousness. Here again, the modern man feels affronted. "How can the righteousness of anyone else be imputed to me?" asks the critic. "It is His righteousness, not mine!"

You have heard, perhaps, about the little boy who was dull at school. He was not only dull with his lessons, he also left much to be desired in his conduct. One day he didn't go to school and his mother said, "Why aren't you going to school?" He answered, "We've got a whole holiday. We've won a scholarship." Notice that he said, "We've won a scholarship." He could have done nothing about it. A lad as dull as he would have been incapable of winning such a scholarship. In the school a clever boy who concentrated had achieved that distinction. And yet, without hesitation and, no doubt, with gratitude, the dull little lad reported, "We've won a scholarship"!

This is only a simple example, but I think it will help you to understand a little of what we mean by imputing righteousness. God permits the purity of Jesus to cover us. The hymn writer puts it like this:

> Jesu, Thy blood and righteousness
> My beauty are, my glorious dress;
> Midst flaming worlds, in these arrayed,
> With joy shall I lift up my head.

No wonder, then, that in all the rapture of a fine hymn Samuel Davies cries out:

> In wonder lost, with trembling joy
> We take the pardon of our God.

And Charles Wesley sings:

> Amazing love! How can it be
> That Thou, my God, shouldst die for me?

In addition to the imputing of righteousness, God likewise imparts it. When any penitent sinner first comes to Him, God imputes His righteousness. Then as we live with Him, He also imparts His righteousness, progressively. It is a part of the Holy Spirit's work to make us holy, too. He sets out not only to justify us, but to sanctify us, and all the time the whole work is by grace. Grace! The free, unmerited favor of God! The grace that today is flowing like a river! The grace to which any needy person in this building may turn with eagerness now!

The Word *Saved*

"By grace are ye saved." Whenever we use the word *saved* some people at once think of hell or heaven. Being saved means to them just that: escaping hell, achieving heaven. But that is a very limited way to think of this term *saved*. For instance, it puts the whole matter in the future. Now we are on earth, not in heaven, and we can be saved now. The Scripture says, "He that believeth on the Son hath eternal life." He has it here and now!

Salvation is not from earth but from sin. It is deliverance not merely from the penalty of sin, but also from the fact of sin. Those of you who are theologically minded may be thinking that I am confusing salvation and sanctification. Still I say that the outworking of salvation gives us deliverance from the sins of the flesh, and likewise from the sins of the mind.

Think of the men who have been hopelessly imprisoned by thirst for strong drink and yet have been delivered from that bondage. Think of the men who have been eaten up with lust, whose heads, in the words of Montaigne, have been "merry-go-rounds of lustful images." Think of people in the grip of greed, who become as metallic as the coins they seek. All of these are victims of present sins, and from these present sins there is for each of them a present salvation.

Not only from the sins of the flesh! There is likewise deliverance from the sins of the mind. From jealousy and all the canker that it brings; from gossip and all the evil that it entails; from pride, the most subtle of sins. From all of these there is salvation, here and now.

Don't, then, think of salvation solely in terms of heaven. Think also in terms of a higher quality of life here on earth. In the light of Christ examine your own heart, and you may find yourself praying like this:

> O God, I am selfish. Too often other folk come second or third in my thoughts. In myself I have discovered jealousy. In the face of some temptations I am terribly weak. I cannot forgive people; I do not truly and deeply forgive. If they speak to me unkindly, hot burning words rush to my lips, and I want to sting them back.
>
> O God, it is hell to live this way at its worst. It must be heaven to be like Christ. If He can get me out of all this and impart to me His quality of life, then I am saved, and He is my Savior.

Have you this quality of life? When you think of Jesus, does the hunger for such a way of living come to you? Do you yearn to be like Him? This is what is in my mind when I think of your being saved. Once again I remind you of this simple truth: "By grace are ye saved."

The Word *Faith*

"By grace are ye saved through faith." Like the word *grace* and the word *saved,* the term *faith* is often misunderstood. Many people agree with the statement of the schoolboy, "Faith is kidding yourself to believe what you know isn't true." Even more elderly and serious commentators regard faith as primarily a matter of the mind.

There are many definitions of faith. No definition can be satisfactory if it confines faith merely to belief. That would make it merely the mental acknowledgment of some external fact and would not include at its very heart the spirit of trust. This is the key word of faith; it means to "trust." Faith is not merely an expression of belief. It is a venture of the whole personality in trusting one who is worthy.

Nor is it right to think, as some people do, that faith belongs only to religion. All life is by faith. When you board a bus you have faith, faith that the driver knows his job. When you go to a restaurant for a meal you have faith, faith that the food is wholesome and well cooked. When you send your child to school you have more faith, faith that the teacher will not poison his mind.

Even science proceeds largely on faith. Contrary to the opinions of some people who haven't thought the matter through, no one can prove the great principles on which scientists proceed, such principles as the uniformity of nature and the conservation of energy. But in order to proceed at all, scientists must assume such basic principles. All business, too, is built on credit. The word *credit* is simply the Latin form of *trust*.

If, then, we find faith everywhere else, should it surprise us to find it also in religion? In common life and in school, in science and in business, we find faith every where. But only in religion do we find it supremely. Just as in the scale of values nothing about a man is so precious as his soul, so the faith through which that soul can be saved must ever be the supreme expression of human trust.

Let me ask, are you conscious of your own need? At the same time are you aware of your weakness, of the pressure of your sins, of the dark problems in your life, and of your inability alone to grapple with them? Do you feel that you need the help of someone else? It is to such felt needs that the Gospel speaks about your being saved.

If you have never yet ventured on Christ, I plead with you to do so now. If you have already received a timorous faith, I urge you to venture on Him far more completely, to recognize that the real end of faith is to unite the person who believes with the person on whom he believes, and that only as you are united with Christ through faith can you have the quality of life that is the sterling of eternity.

This is the glad, good news that the evangelists carried everywhere in the first century and that their true followers have echoed in all the centuries since. Our Wesleyan fathers sounded it with tremendous power in the eighteenth century. In an age when most people had lost all hope, when they mistakenly thought that God was not there or that He was not kind, the spokesmen for God came with the burning message that He was there and that He was kind; that by His free generosity men could be lifted into fullness of life, if only they trusted in Christ. This is still the heart of the Gospel. I sound it again, with jubilation.

Nineteen hundred years after the apostles first proclaimed this Gospel and more than two hundred years after John Wesley first received it in his heart, I again offer you this Gospel: "By grace are ye saved through faith."

Grace Abounding Over Abounding Sin

Charles Haddon Spurgeon (1834–1892) is undoubtedly the most famous minister of the nineteenth century. Converted in 1850, he united with the Baptists and soon began to preach in various places. He became pastor of the Baptist church in Waterbeach, England, in 1851, and three years later he was called to the decaying Park Street Church, London. Within a short time the work began to prosper, a new church was built and dedicated in 1861, and Spurgeon became London's most popular preacher. In 1855, he began to publish his sermons weekly; today they make up the fifty-seven volumes of *The Metropolitan Tabernacle Pulpit*. He founded a pastor's college and several orphanages.

This sermon is taken from *The Metropolitan Tabernacle Pulpit*, volume 34.

Charles Haddon Spurgeon

11

GRACE ABOUNDING OVER ABOUNDING SIN

Moreover the law entered, that the offence might abound. But where sin abounded, grace did much more abound (Romans 5:20).

THE FIRST SENTENCE will serve as a preface; the second sentence will be the actual text.

"Moreover the law entered, that the offence might abound." Man was a sinner before the law of Ten Commandments had been given. He was a sinner through the offense of his first father, Adam. He was also practically a sinner by his own personal offense, for he rebelled against the light of nature and the inner light of conscience. Men, from Adam downward, transgressed against that memory of better days which had been handed down from father to son and had never been quite forgotten. Man everywhere, whether he knew anything about the Law of Moses or not, was alienated from his God. The Word of God contains this truthful estimate of our race: "They are all gone out of the way, they are together become unprofitable; there is none that doeth good, no, not one."

The law was given, however, according to the text, "that the offence might abound." Such was the effect of the law. It did not hinder sin nor provide a remedy for it, but its actual effect was that the offense abounded. How so?

It was so, first, because it revealed the offense. Men did not in every instance clearly discern what was sin. But when the law came, it pointed out to man that this evil, which he thought little of, was as abomination in the sight of God. Man's nature and character was like a dark dungeon that knew no ray of light. Yonder prisoner does not perceive the horrible filthiness and corruption of the place wherein he is immured, so long as he is in darkness. When a lamp is brought or a window is opened and the light of day comes in, he finds out to his dismay the hideous condition of his den. He spies loathsome creatures upon the walls and marks how others burrow out of sight because the light annoys them. He may, perhaps, have guessed that all was not as it should be, but he had not imagined the abundance of the evils. The light has entered, and the offense abounds. Law does not make us sinful, but it displays our sinfulness. In the presence of the perfect standard we see our shortcomings. The law of God is the looking glass in which a man sees the spots upon his face. It does not wash you—you cannot wash in a looking glass—but it prompts you to seek the cleansing water. The design of the law is the revealing of our many offenses that, thereby, we may be driven out of self-righteousness to the Lord Jesus, in whom we have redemption through His blood, the forgiveness of sin.

The law causes the offense to abound by making an offender to stand without excuse. Before he knew the law perfectly, his sin was not so willful. While he did but faintly know the commands, he could, as it were, but faintly break them, but as soon as he distinctly knows what is right and what is wrong, then every cloak is taken away from him. Sin becomes exceeding sinful when it is committed against light and knowledge. Is it not so with some of you? Are you not forced to admit that you commit many sins in one, now that you have been made to know the law and yet willfully offend against it by omission or commission? He who knows his Master's will and does it not will be beaten with many stripes because he is guilty of abounding offenses. The law enters to strip us of every cloak of justification and so to drive us to seek the robe of Christ's righteousness.

Next, I think the law makes the offense to abound by causing sin to be more evidently a presumptuous rebellion against the great Lawgiver. To sin in the front of Sinai, with its wonderful display of divine majesty, is to sin indeed. To rebel against a law promulgated with sound of trumpet and thunders and pomp of God is to sin with a high hand and a defiant heart. When you have heard the Ten Commandments, when you know the law of the kingdom, when your Maker's will is plainly set before you, then to transgress is to transgress with an insolence of pride that will admit of no excuse.

Once more: the entrance of the law makes the offense to abound in this sense, that the rebellious will of man rises up in opposition to it. Because God commands, man refuses; because He forbids, man desires. There are some men who might not have sinned in a particular direction if the commandment had not forbidden it. The light of the law, instead of being a warning to them to avoid evil, seems to point out to them the way in which they can most offend. Oh, how deep is the depravity of human nature! The law itself provokes it to rebel. Men long to enter because trespassers are warned to keep away. Their minds are so at enmity against God that they delight in that which is forbidden not so much because they find any particular pleasure in the thing itself but because it shows their independence and their freedom from the restraints of God. This vicious self-will is in all of us by nature, for the carnal mind is enmity against God. Therefore the law, though in itself holy and just and good, provokes us to do evil. We are like lime, and the law is as cold water, which is in itself of a cooling nature. Yet, no sooner does the water of the law get at the lime of human nature than a heat of sin is generated. Thus, "the law entered, that the offence might abound."

Why, then, did God send the law? Is it not an evil thing that the offense should abound? In itself it may seem so to be, but God deals with us as physicians sometimes deal with their patients. A disease that will be fatal if it spends itself within the patient must be brought to the surface. The physician therefore prescribes a medicine that displays the evil. The evil was all within, but it did not abound as to its visible effects. It is needful that it should do so that it may be cured. The law is the medicine that throws out the depravity of man, makes him see it in his actions, and even provokes him to display it. The evil is in man like rabbits in yonder brushwood. The law sets a light to the cover and the hidden creatures are seen. The law stirs the mud at the bottom of the pool and proves how foul the waters are. The law compels the man to see that sin dwells in him and that it is a powerful tyrant over his nature. All this is with a view to his cure. God be thanked when the law so works as to take off the sinner from all confidence in himself! To make the leper confess that he is incurable is going a great way toward compelling him to go to that divine Savior who alone is able to heal him. This is the object and end of the law toward men whom God will save.

Consider for a moment. You may take it as an axiom, a thing self-evident, that there can be no grace where there is no guilt; there can be no mercy where there is no sin. There can be justice, there can be benevolence, but there cannot be mercy unless there is criminality. If you are not a sinner God cannot have mercy upon you. If you have never sinned God cannot display pardoning grace toward you, for there is nothing to pardon. It were a misuse of words to talk of forgiving a man who has done no wrong or to speak of bestowing undeserved favor upon a person who deserves reward. It would be an insult to innocence to offer it mercy. You must, therefore, have sin or you cannot have grace—that is clear.

Next, consider that there will be no seeking after grace where there is no sense of sin. We may preach until we are hoarse, but you good people who have never broken the law and are not guilty of anything wrong will never care for our message of mercy. You are such kind people that, out of compliment to religion, you say, "Yes, we are sinners. We are all sinners." But you know in your heart of hearts you do not mean it. You will never ask for grace, for you have no sense of shame or guilt. None of you will seek mercy until first you have pleaded guilty to the indictment that the law of God presents against you. Oh, that you felt your sins! Oh, that you knew your need of forgiveness! For then you would see yourselves to be in such a condition that only the free, rich, sovereign grace of God can save you.

Furthermore, I am sure that there will be no reception and acceptance of grace by any man until there is a full confession of sin and a burdensome sense of its weight. Why should you receive grace when you do not want it? What is the use of it to you? Why should you bow your knee to God and receive, as the free gift of His charity, that which you feel you deserve? Have you not already earned eternal life? Are you not as good as other people? Have you not some considerable claim upon God? Do I startle you with these plain questions? Have I not heard you say much the same? The other day when we preached the electing love of God, you grumbled and muttered that God was unjust to choose one rather than another. What did this mean? Did it not mean that you felt you had some claim upon God? O sir, if this is your spirit, I must deal plainly with you! If you have any claim upon your Maker, plead it, and be sure that He will not deny you your just rights. But I would advise you to change your method of dealing with your judge. You will never prevail in this fashion. In truth, you have no claim upon Him but must appeal to His pure mercy. You are not in a position for Him to display free grace to you until your mouth is shut and you sit down in dust and ashes, silently owning that you deserve nothing at His hands but infinite displeasure. Confess that whatever He gives you that is good and gracious must be given freely to one who deserves nothing. Hell gapes at your feet; cease from pride and humbly sue out a pardon.

You see, then, the use of the law: it is to bring you where grace can be fitly shown you. It shuts you up that you may cry to Jesus to set you free. It is a storm that wrecks your hopes of self-salvation but washes you upon the Rock of Ages. The condemning sentence of the law is meant to prepare you for the absolution of the Gospel. If you condemn yourself and plead guilty before God, the royal pardon can then be extended toward you. The self-condemned shall be forgiven through the precious blood of Jesus and the sovereign grace of God. Oh, my hearer, you must sit down there in the dust or else God will not look at you! You must yield yourself to Him, owning His justice, honoring His law. This is the first condition of His mercy, and to this His grace brings all who feel its power. The Lord will have you bow before Him in self-abhorrence and confess His right to punish you. Remember, He will have mercy on whom he will have mercy, and he will have compassion on whom he will have compassion. He will have you know this and agree to it. His grace must reign triumphantly, and you must kiss its silver scepter.

Thus has the first sentence served us for a preface. God bless it to us!

The doctrine of the text itself is this, that "where sin abounded, grace did much more abound." I shall try to bring out that truth.

This Is Seen in the Whole Work of Grace

I would direct your attention to the context. The safest way to preach upon a text is to follow out the idea that the inspired writer was endeavoring to convey. Paul, in this place, has been speaking of the abounding result for evil of one sin in the case of Adam, the federal head of the race. That one sin of Adam's abounded terribly. Look at the multitudinous generations of our race that have gone down to death. Who slew all these? Sin is the wolf that has devoured the flocks of men. Sin has poisoned the streams of manhood at their fountainhead, and everywhere they run with poisoned waters. Concerning this, Paul says, "Where sin abounded, grace did much more abound."

First, then, *sin abounded in its effect upon the whole human race.* One sin overthrew all humanity; one fatal fault, the breach of a plain and easy law, made sinners of us all. "By one man's disobedience many were made sinners." Simple as was the command that Adam broke, it involved obedience or disobedience to the sovereignty of God. All the trees of the garden were generously given to happy Adam in Paradise: "Of every tree of the garden thou mayest freely eat." There was but one tree reserved for God by the prohibition, "Thou shalt not eat of it: for in the day that thou eatest thereof thou shalt surely die." Adam had no need to touch that fruit, there were all the other trees for him. Nothing was denied him that was really for his good; he was only forbidden that which would ruin him. We all look back to that Paradisaical state and wish we could have been put in some such a position as he. Yet he dared to trespass on God's reserves and thus to set himself up above his Maker. He judged it wise to do what God forbade. He ran the risk of death in the foolish hope of rising into a still higher state.

See the consequences of that sin on all sides; the world is full of them. Yet, says Paul, "Where sin abounded, grace did much more abound." He gives us this as a proof of it: "And not as it was by one that sinned, so is the gift: for the judgment was by one to condemnation, but the free gift is of many offences unto justification" (Rom. 5:16). The Lord Jesus came into the world not alone to put away Adam's sin but all the sins that have followed upon it. The second Adam has repaired the desperate ruin of the first, and much more. By His death upon the cross, our Divine Substitute has put away those myriads of sins that have been committed by men since the first offense in Eden. Think of this! Take the whole aggregate of believers and let each one disburden his conscience of its load of sin. What a mountain! Pile it up! Pile it up! It rises huge as high Olympus! Age after age believers come and lay their enormous loads in this place. "The Lord hath made to meet on him the iniquities of us all." What Alps! What Himalayas of sin! If there were only mine and yours, my brother, what mountains of division would our sins make! But the great Christ, the free gift of God to us, when He bare our sins in His own body on the tree, took all those countless sins away. "Behold the Lamb of God, which taketh away the sin of the world"! Here is infinite grace to pardon immeasurable sin! Truly the "one man's offence" abounded horribly, but the "one man's obedience," the obedience of the Son of God, has superabounded. As the arch of heaven far exceeds in its span the whole round globe of the earth, so does grace much more abound over human sin.

Follow me further, when I notice, secondly, that *sin abounded in its ruinous effects.* It utterly destroyed humanity. In the third chapter of Romans you see how, in every part of his nature, man is depraved by sin. Think of the havoc that the tyrant, sin, has made of our natural estate and heritage. Eden is withered—its very site is forgotten. Our restfulness among the trees of the field, freely yielding their fruit, is gone, and God has said, "In the sweat of thy face shalt thou eat bread." The field we till has lost its spontaneous yield of corn: "Thorns also and thistles shall it bring forth to thee." Life has lost its glory and immortality, for "Dust thou art, and unto dust shalt thou return." Every woman in her pangs of travail, every man in his weariness of labor, and all of us together in the griefs of death see what sin has done for us as to our mortal bodies. Alas, it has gone deeper; it has ruined our souls. Sin has unmanned man. The crown and glory of his manhood it has thrown to the ground. All our faculties are out of gear; all our tendencies are perverted. Beloved, let us rejoice that the Lord Jesus Christ has come to redeem us from the curse of sin, and He will undo the evil of evil. Even this poor world He will deliver from the bondage of corruption. He will create new heavens and a new earth wherein dwells righteousness. The groans and painful travail of the whole creation shall result in a full deliverance and somewhat more through the grace of our Lord Jesus Christ. As for ourselves, we are lifted up to a position far higher than that which we should have occupied had the race continued in its innocence.

The Lord Jesus Christ found us in a horrible pit and in the miry clay, and He not only lifted us up out of it, but He set our feet upon a rock and established our goings. Raised from hell, we are lifted not to the bowers of Eden but to the throne of God. Redeemed human nature has greater capacities than unfallen human nature. To Adam the Lord did not say, Thou art a son of God, joint heir with the Only Begotten, but He has said that to each believer redeemed by the precious blood of Jesus. Beloved, such a thing as fellowship with Christ in His sufferings could not have been known to Adam in Paradise. He could not have known what it is to be dead and to have his life hid with Christ in God. Blessed be His name, our Lord Jesus Christ can say, "I restored that which I took not away"! He restored more than ever was taken away from us. He has made us to be partakers of the divine nature, and in His own person He has placed us at God's right hand in the heavenly places. Inasmuch as the dominion of the Lord Jesus is more glorious than that of unfallen Adam, manhood is now more great and glorious than before the Fall. Grace has so much more abounded that in Jesus we have gained more than in Adam we lost. Our Paradise Regained is far more glorious than our Paradise Lost.

Again, *sin abounded to the dishonor of God.* I was trying the other day to put myself into the position of Satan at the gates of Eden that I might understand his diabolical policy. He had become the archenemy of God. When he saw this newly made world and perceived two perfectly pure and happy creatures placed in it, he looked on with envy and plotted mischief. He heard the Creator say, "In the day that thou eatest thereof thou shalt surely die," and he hoped here to find an opportunity for an assault upon God. If he could induce those new-made creatures to eat of the forbidden fruit, he would place their Maker upon the horns of a dilemma: either He must destroy the creatures that He had made, or else He must be untrue. The Lord had said, "Thou shalt surely die." He must thus undo His own work and destroy a creature that He had made in His own image, after His own likeness. Satan, probably, perceived that man was an extraordinary being with a wonderful mystery of glory hanging about his destiny. If he could make him sin he would cause God to destroy him and so far defeat the eternal purpose. On the other hand, if the Lord did not execute the sentence, then He would not be truthful, and throughout all His great universe it would be reported that the Lord's word had been broken. Either He had changed His mind or He had spoken in jest or He had been proven to have threatened too severe a penalty. In either case, the evil spirit hoped to triumph. It was a deep, far-reaching scheme to dim the splendor of the King of Kings.

Beloved, did it not seem as if sin had abounded beyond measure, when first the woman and then the man had been deceived and had done despite to God? Behold how grace, through our Lord Jesus Christ, did much more abound! God is more honored in the redemption of man than if there had never been a Fall. The Lord has displayed the majesty of His justice and the glory of His grace in the great sacrifice of His dear Son in such a manner that angels and principalities and powers will wonder throughout all ages. More of God is to be seen in the great work of redeeming love than could have been reflected in the creation of myriads of worlds had each one of them been replete with marvels of divine skill and goodness and power. In Jesus crucified, Jehovah is glorified as never before. Where sin abounded to the apparent dishonor of God, grace does much more abound to the infinite glory of His ever-blessed name.

Again, *sin abounded by degrading human character.* What a wretched being man is as a sinner against God! Unchecked by law and allowed to do as he pleases, what will not man become? See how Paul describes men in these progressive times—in these enlightened centuries: "This know also, that in the last days perilous times shall come. For men shall be lovers of their own selves, covetous, boasters, proud, blasphemers, disobedient to parents, unthankful, unholy, without natural affection, trucebreakers, false accusers, incontinent, fierce, despisers of those that are good, traitors, heady, highminded, lovers of pleasures more than lovers of God; having a form of godliness, but denying the power thereof." Human nature was not at all slandered by Whitefield when he said that, "left to himself, man is half beast and half devil." I do not mean merely men in savage countries—I am thinking of men in London. Only the other day a certain newspaper gave us plenty of proof of the sin of this city. I will say no more—could brutes or demons be worse? Read human history, Assyrian, Roman, Greek, Saracenic, Spanish, English, and if you are a lover of holiness, you will be sick of man. Has any other creature, except the fallen angels, ever become so cruel, so mean, so false? Behold what villains, what tyrants, what monsters sin has made!

But now look on the other side, and see what the grace of God has done. Under the molding hand of the Holy Spirit, a gracious man becomes the noblest work of God. Man, born again and rescued from the Fall, is now capable of virtues to which he never could have reached before he sinned. An unfallen being could not hate sin with the intensity of abhorrence that is found in the renewed heart. We now know by personal experience the horror of sin, and there is now within us an instinctive shuddering at it. An unfallen being could not exhibit patience, for it could not suffer, and patience has its perfect work to do. When I have read the stories of the martyrs in the first ages of the Christian church and during the Marian persecution in England, I have adored the Lord who could enable poor feeble men and women thus to prove their love to their God and Savior. What great things they suffered out of love to God and how grandly did they thus honor him! O God, what a noble being your grace has made man to be! I have felt great reverence for sanctified humanity when I have seen how men could sing God's praises in the fires. What noble deeds men have been capable of when the love of

God has been shed abroad in their hearts! I do not think angels or archangels have ever been able to exhibit so admirable an all-round character as the grace of God has wrought in once-fallen men whom He has, by His grace, inspired with the divine life. In human character, "where sin abounded, grace did much more abound." I believe God looks out of heaven today and sees in many of His poor, hidden people such beauties of virtue, such charms of holiness, that He Himself is delighted with them. "The LORD taketh pleasure in them that fear him." These are such true jewels that the Lord has a high estimate of them and sets them apart for himself: "They shall be mine, saith the LORD of hosts, in that day when I make up my jewels."

Again, dear friends, *sin abounded to the causing of great sorrow.* It brought with it a long train of woes. The children of sin are many, and each one causes lamentation. We cannot attempt to fathom the dark abysses of sorrow that have opened in this world since the advent of sin. Is it not a place of fears—yes, a field of blood? Yet by a wonderful alchemy, through the existence of sin, grace has produced a new joy, yes, more than one new joy. The calm, deep joy of repentance must have been unknown to perfect innocence. This right orient pearl is not found in the rivers of Eden. Yes, and that joy which is in heaven in the presence of the angels of God over sinners that repent is a new thing whose birth is since the Fall. God Himself knows a joy that He could not have known had there been no sin. Behold, with tearful wonder, the great Father as He receives His returning prodigal and cries to all about Him, "Let us eat, and be merry: for this my son was dead, and is alive again; he was lost, and is found." O brethren, how could almighty love have been victorious in grace had there been no sin to battle with? Heaven is the more heaven for us since there we shall sing of robes washed white in the blood of the Lamb. God has greater joy in man, and man has greater joy in God, because grace abounded over sin. We are getting into deep waters now! How true our text is!

Once more, *sin abounded to hinder the reign of Christ.* I believe that Satan's design in leading men into sin at the first was to prevent the supremacy of the Lord Jesus Christ as man and God in one person. I do not lay it down as a doctrine specifically taught in Scripture, but still it seems to me a probable truth, that Satan foresaw that the gap that was made in heaven by the fall of the angels was to be filled up by human beings whom God would place near His throne. Satan thought that he saw before him the beings who would take the places of the fallen spirits, and he envied them. He knew that they were made in the image of the Only Begotten, the Christ of God, and he hated Him because he saw united in His person God whom he abhorred and man whom he envied. Satan shot at the second Adam through the breast of the first Adam. Fool that he was, he meant to overthrow the Coming One. But the Lord Jesus Christ, by the grace of God, is now exalted higher than ever we could conceive Him to have been had there been no sin to bear, no redemption to work out. Jesus, wounded and slain, has about Him higher splendor than before. King of Kings and Lord of Lords, Man of Sorrows, we sing hallelujahs to You! All our hearts beat true to You! We love You beyond all else! You are He whom we will praise forever and ever! Jesus sits on no precarious throne in the empire of love. We would each one maintain His right with the last pulse of our hearts. King of Kings and Lord of Lords! Hallelujah! Where sin abounded, grace has much more abounded to the glory of the only begotten Son of God.

I find time always flies fastest when our subject is most precious. I have a second head that deserves a lengthened consideration, but we must be content with mere hints. This great fact, that where sin abounded, grace did much more abound, crops up everywhere.

This Is to Be Seen in Special Cases

The first special case is *the introduction of the law.* When the law of Ten Commandments was given through man's sin, it ministered to the abounding of the offense, but it also ministered to the abounding of grace. It is true there were ten commands, but there was more than tenfold grace. With the law there came forward a High Priest. The world had never seen a high priest before, arrayed in jeweled breastplate and garments of glory and beauty. There was the law, but at the same time there was the Holy Place of the tabernacle of the Most High with its altar, its laver, its candlestick, and its table of show bread. There was, also, the secret shrine where the majesty of God dwelt. God had, by those symbols and types, come to dwell among men. It is true, sin abounded through the law; but, then, sacrifices for sin also abounded. Heretofore, there had been no morning and evening lambs; there had been no Day of Atonement, no sprinkling of blood, no benediction from the Lord's high priest. For every sin that the law revealed, a sacrifice was provided. Sins of ignorance, sins of their holy things, sins of all sorts were met by special sacrifices so that the sins uncovered to the conscience were also covered by the sacrifice.

The story of Israel is another case in point. How often the nation rebelled, but how often did mercy rejoice over judgment! Truly the history of the chosen people shows how sin abounded and grace did much more abound.

Run your eye down history and pause at *the crucifixion of our Lord Jesus*. This is the highest peak of the mountains of sin. They crucified the Lord of glory. Here sin abounded. But do I need to tell you that grace did here much more abound? You can look at the death of Christ until Pilate vanishes and Caiaphas fades away and all the clamor of the priests and Jews is hushed, and you see nothing and hear nothing but free grace and dying love.

There followed upon the crucifixion of our Lord *the casting away of the Jewish people for a while.* Sin abounded when the Lord thus came to His own and His own received Him not. Yes, but the casting away of them was the saving of the nations. "We turn to the Gentiles," said the apostle, and that was a blessed turning for you and for me. Was it not? They that were bidden to the feast were not worthy, and the master of the house, being angry, invited other guests. Mark, "being angry"! What did He do when He was angry? Why, He did the most gracious thing of all; He said, "Go out into the highways and hedges," and as many as you shall find bid to the supper. Sin abounded, for Israel would not enter the feast of love, but grace did much more abound, for the heathen entered the kingdom.

The heathen world at that time was sunk in the blackest darkness, and sin abounded. You have only to study ancient history and you will fetch a heavy sigh to think that men could be so vile. A poor and unlettered people were chosen of God to receive the Gospel of Jesus, and they went about telling of an atoning Savior, in their own simple way, until the Roman Empire was entirely changed. Light and peace and truth came into the world and drove away slavery and tyranny and bestial lust. Where sin abounded, grace did much more abound. What wonderful characters were produced in the terrible reign of Diocletian! What consecration to God was seen in the confessors! What fearlessness in common Christians! What invincible loyalty to Christ in the martyrs! Out of barbarians the Lord made saints, and the degraded rose to holiness sublime.

If I were to ask you, now, to give the best illustrations of grace abounding in individuals, I think your impulse would be to choose *men in whom sin once abounded*. What characters do we preach of most when we would magnify the grace of God? We talk of David, and Manasseh and swearing Peter and the dying thief, and Saul of Tarsus and the woman that was a sinner. If we want to show where grace abounded, we naturally turn our eyes to the place where sin abounded. Is it not so? Therefore, I need not give you any more cases—it is proven that where sin abounded, grace did much more abound.

This Holds True to Each One of Us

Lastly, and this is what I want to hold you to, dear friends, at this time: let me take the case of *the open sinner*. What have you been? Have you grossly sinned? Have you defiled your body with unhallowed passions? Have you been dishonest to your fellowmen? Does some scarlet sin stain your conscience even as you sit in the pew? Have you grown hardened in sin by long perseverance in it? Are you conscious that you have frequently, willfully, and resolutely sinned? Are you getting old, and have you been soaking these seventy years in the crimson dye of sin until you are saturated through and through with its color? Have you even been an implacable opponent of the Gospel? Have you persecuted the saints of God? Have you tried by argument to batter down the Gospel or by ridicule to put it to reproach? Then hear this text: "Where sin abounded, grace did much more abound"; as it was in the beginning, it is now and ever shall be, until this world shall end. The grace of God, if you believe in the Lord Jesus Christ, will triumph over the greatness of your wickedness. "All manner of sin and blasphemy shall be forgiven unto men." Throw down your weapons of rebellion; surrender at discretion, kiss the pierced hand of Jesus that is now held out to you, and this very moment you shall be forgiven and shall go your way a pardoned man to begin a new life and to bear witness that "where sin abounded, grace did much more abound."

Perhaps this does not touch you, my friend. Listen to my next word, which is addressed to *the instructed sinner*. You are a person whose religious education has made you aware of the guilt of sin. You have read your Bible and have heard truthful preaching. Although you have never been a gross open sinner, yet you know that your life teems with sins of omission and commission. You know that you have sinned against light and knowledge. You have done despite to a tender conscience very often; therefore you rightly judge that you are even a greater sinner than the more openly profane. Be it so; I take you at that. Do not run back from it. Let it be so, for "where sin abounded, grace did much more abound." Oh, that you may be as much instructed in the remedy as you are instructed in the disease! Oh, that you may have as clear a view of the righteousness of Christ as you have of your own unrighteousness! Christ's work is a divine work, broad enough to cover all your iniquity and to conquer all your sin. Believe this! Give glory to God by believing it, and according to your faith, so be it to you.

I address another who does not answer either of these two descriptions exactly, but he has lately begun to seek mercy, and the more he prays the more he is *tempted*. Horrible suggestions rush into his mind—damnable thoughts beset and bewilder him. Ah, my friend, I know what this means: the nearer you are to mercy, the nearer you seem to get to hell-gate! When you most solemnly mean to do good you feel another law in your members bringing you into captivity. You grow worse where you hoped you would have grown better. Very well, then, grip my text firmly as for your life: "Where sin abounded, grace did much more abound." If a whole legion of devils should be let loose upon you, Christ will glorify Himself by mastering them all. If now you cannot repent nor pray nor do anything, remember that text, "When we were yet without strength, in due time Christ died for the ungodly." Look over the heads of all these doubts and devils and inabilities, and see Jesus lifted on the cross like the brazen serpent upon the pole. Look to Him and the fiery serpents shall flee away from you, and you shall live. Believe this text to be true, for true it is: "Where sin abounded, grace did much more abound."

"Ah!" says another, "my case is still worse, sir. I am of a *despondent* turn of mind. I always look upon the black side of every thing. Now if I read a promise, I am sure it is not for me. If I see a threatening in God's Word, I am sure it is for me. I have no hope. I do not seem as if I should ever have any. I am in a dungeon into which no light can enter. It is dark, dark, dark, and worse darkness is coming. While you are trying to comfort me, I put the comfort away." I know you. You are like the poor creature in the psalm of whom we read: His "soul abhorreth all manner of meat." Even the Gospel itself he cannot relish. Yes; I know you. You are writing bitter things against yourself. This morning you have been newly dipping your pen in gall, but your writing is that of a poor bewildered creature. It is not to be taken notice of. I see you writing, in text hand, great black words of condemnation, but there is nothing in them all. Verily, verily I say to you, your handwriting shall be blotted out, and the curse, causeless, shall not come. Thus says the Lord, "Your covenant with death shall be disannulled, and your agreement with hell shall not stand, for the Lord Jesus Christ has redeemed you, and where sin abounded, grace shall much more abound." Broken in pieces, all asunder, ground between the millstones, reduced to nothing, yet believe this revelation of God that where sin abounded, grace did much more abound. Notice that "much more"—"much more abound." If you cannot grip it and know it to be of a certainty the great principle upon which God acts, that grace shall outstrip sin, then there is hope of you. No, more than hope, there is salvation for you on the spot. If you believe in Jesus, whom God has set forth to be a propitiation for sin, you are forgiven.

Oh, my hearers, do not despise this grace! Come, and partake of it. Does anyone say, as Paul foresaw that some would say, "Let us sin, that grace may abound"? Ah, then, such an infamous inference is the mark of the reprobate, and your damnation is just. He that turns God's mercy into a reason for sin has within him something worse than a heart of stone. Surely his conscience is seared with a hot iron. Beloved, I hope better things of you. I trust that, on the contrary, the sound of the silver bells of infinite love, free pardon, abounding grace, will make you hasten to the hospital of mercy that you may receive healing for your sinfulness, strength for your feebleness, and joy for your sorrow. Lord, grant that in this house, in every case wherein sin has abounded, grace may yet more abound, for Jesus' sake! Amen.